HOT TOPICS

ANIMAL RIGHTS

A COMPLEX DEBATE

By Tyler Stevenson

Portions of this book originally appeared in *Animal Rights* by Karen D. Povey.

LUCENT
PRESS

Published in 2019 by
Lucent Press, an Imprint of Greenhaven Publishing, LLC
353 3rd Avenue
Suite 255
New York, NY 10010

Designer: Deanna Paternostro
Editor: Jennifer Lombardo

Library of Congress Cataloging-in-Publication Data

Names: Stevenson, Tyler (Tyler Dennis), 1988- author.
Title: Animal rights : a complex debate / Tyler Stevenson.
Description: First Edition. | New York : Lucent Press, [2019] | Series: Hot topics | Includes index.
Identifiers: LCCN 2018024919 (print) | LCCN 2018029116 (ebook) | ISBN 9781534565012 (eBook) | ISBN 9781534565364 (library bound book) | ISBN 9781534565005 (pbk. book)
Subjects: LCSH: Animal rights.
Classification: LCC HV4708 (ebook) | LCC HV4708 .S658 2019 (print) | DDC 179/.3–dc23
LC record available at https://lccn.loc.gov/2018024919

Printed in the United States of America

CPSIA compliance information: Batch #BW19KL: For further information contact Greenhaven Publishing LLC, New York, New York at 1-844-317-7404.

Please visit our website, www.greenhavenpublishing.com. For a free color catalog of all our high-quality books, call toll free 1-844-317-7404 or fax 1-844-317-7405.

CONTENTS

FOREWORD

Adolescence is a time when many people begin to take notice of the world around them. News channels, blogs, and talk radio shows are constantly promoting one view or another; very few are unbiased. Young people also hear conflicting information from parents, friends, teachers, and acquaintances. Often, they will hear only one side of an issue or be given flawed information. People who are trying to support a particular viewpoint may cite inaccurate facts and statistics on their blogs, and news programs present many conflicting views of important issues in our society. In a world where it seems everyone has a platform to share their thoughts, it can be difficult to find unbiased, accurate information about important issues.

It is not only facts that are important. In blog posts, in comments on online videos, and on talk shows, people will share opinions that are not necessarily true or false, but can still have a strong impact. For example, many young people struggle with their body image. Seeing or hearing negative comments about particular body types online can have a huge effect on the way someone views himself or herself and may lead to depression and anxiety. Although it is important not to keep information hidden from young people under the guise of protecting them, it is equally important to offer encouragement on issues that affect their mental health.

The titles in the Hot Topics series provide readers with different viewpoints on important issues in today's society. Many of these issues, such as domestic abuse and free speech rights online, are of immediate concern to young people. This series aims to give readers factual context on these crucial topics in a way that lets them form their own opinions. The facts presented throughout also serve to empower readers to help themselves or support people they know who are struggling with many of the challenges adolescents face today. Although negative viewpoints are not ignored or downplayed, this series allows young people to see that the challenges they face are not insurmountable. Abusive relationships can be ended, the internet can be navigated safely, and the environment can be saved.

Quotes encompassing all viewpoints are presented and cited so readers can trace them back to their original source, verifying for themselves whether the information comes from a reputable place. Additional books and websites are listed, giving readers a starting point from which to continue their own research. Chapter questions encourage discussion, allowing young people to hear and understand their classmates' points of view as they further solidify their own. Full-color photographs and enlightening charts provide a deeper understanding of the topics at hand. All of these features augment the informative text, helping young people understand the world they live in and formulate their own opinions concerning the best way they can improve it.

INTRODUCTION

Understanding the Controversy

For as many years as humanity has existed, people have shared the world with various species of animals, and society's interactions with and attitudes toward animals have been evolving ever since. The span of human history is miniscule compared to that of most other species, some of which have long since become extinct and others of which have evolved into the more recognizable species people live with today.

At first, animals were seen mainly as a source of food. Prehistoric people killed and ate animals long before they had the basic technology or knowledge to create hunting tools or the ability to cook the meat of the animals they killed. Many years later, humans began domesticating certain species of animals, both to use as labor and as easily farmed food sources. They discovered it was much easier to kill and eat a tame animal that had been raised and kept specifically for that purpose than it was to try to track down and kill a wild one.

For most of human history, animals have generally been seen as property, useful only for what they could provide in terms of food, labor, and clothing. Even today, this is a popular opinion, as people often argue about what can be considered consciousness in an animal. Some people believe that only creatures with a very high level of self-awareness and intelligence are deserving of any kinds of rights, which essentially limits these rights to only human beings.

As people gathered more and more in cities, the use of animals as pets and companions increased, as it is typically not necessary to have beasts of labor or animals for personal food sources in urban areas. People began keeping domesticated dogs and cats, among other species, solely for comfort and companionship. Today, many people treat cats and dogs as members of their families, caring for them and taking them to expensive veterinarian appointments to keep them healthy and happy.

Today, animals are often treated as beloved members of the family.

As people moved off farms and into cities and began keeping animals as pets, attitudes toward animals began to change. Even as far back as the late 1700s, people began to oppose the often poor treatment of animals, arguing that they should not be treated cruelly and that they should be given some form of rights. In 1776, British Reverend Humphrey Primatt expressed the opinion that animals should be treated with compassion, writing, "See that no brute of any kind ... whether intrusted to thy care, or coming in thy way, suffer thy neglect or abuse. Let no views of profit, no compliance with custom, and no fear of ridicule of the world, ever tempt thee to the least act of cruelty or injustice to any creature whatsoever."[1] This was a fairly radical concept at the time, and not an especially widespread belief.

In recent years, the concept of animal rights has become increasingly popular. The idea of basic animal welfare, such as the idea that animals should not be abused or beaten, is generally accepted by a vast majority of people. More narrowly held—but gaining traction in modern society—is the idea that animals should not be used for clothing, food, or any of the other traditional uses people have kept animals for throughout history.

Various animal rights activist groups have used different tactics in their attempt to end the use of animals entirely—from the relatively harmless, celebrity-driven attempts of organizations such as People for the Ethical Treatment of Animals (PETA) to the more militant, aggressive tactics of the Animal Liberation Front (ALF). Animal rights activists have been praised and condemned in equal measure, and there are still varying degrees of opinions on exactly what rights animals deserve. It is generally accepted that animals should not be abused or treated cruelly, but the more extreme idea of ending animal use entirely is not widespread among the general population.

Animal Rights

Animal rights are not seen in the same way as human rights. Since animals cannot speak, people tend to think of them as lesser creatures and are quite comfortable owning them. The fact that humans can own animals makes them, in many people's opinions, property. People kill and eat farm animals; hunt wild animals, both for food and trophies; force animals to participate in things humans consider sports, such as horse racing; and capture and imprison them, displaying them in zoos. All of these activities are currently legal, although over time, society has established many laws to ensure that these are done as humanely as possible.

French philosopher René Descarte, in his 1641 work "Meditations," presented the concept of animals as complex mechanisms, with no souls, minds, or ability to reason. This was the prevailing attitude at the time and shaped human interaction with animals well into the 20th century.

Other philosophers argued against the cruel treatment of animals, not for the sake of the animal itself, but believing that performing acts of cruelty damaged the human soul. English philosopher John Locke wrote in 1693 that unnecessary cruelty toward animals was wrong because an animal that was constantly mistreated would eventually hurt a person. German philosopher Immanuel Kant expanded on this idea in 1785, writing, "Cruelty to animals is contrary to man's duty to *himself*, because it deadens in him the feeling of sympathy for their sufferings, and thus a natural tendency that is very useful to morality in relation to other human beings is weakened."[2]

One of the first major pieces of animal rights legislation was passed in Ireland in 1822. An Act to Prevent the Cruel and

Improper Treatment of Cattle, or "Martin's Act," as it became known, made it an offense to "beat, abuse, or ill-treat any horse, mare, gelding, mule, ass, ox, cow, heifer, steer, sheep, or other cattle."[3] This was an offense punishable by a fine up to 5 pounds—the currency in the United Kingdom, which Ireland was part of at the time—or two months' imprisonment. This was a huge amount of money at the time; in today's currency, 5 pounds would be about 580 pounds, which is equal to about 810 United States dollars (USD). Various similar laws were passed soon after that in other countries throughout the world.

Although this act was passed, the bill's namesake, Richard Martin, a member of Parliament (MP) for Galway in Ireland, found that it was not being taken seriously, and the fines and punishments for violation of the law were not being applied consistently by local magistrates (British officials who enforced laws). However, it had gained traction among various social reformers such as Reverend Arthur Broome, who, together with a group of like-minded people, sought to create an organization that would work to prevent cruelty toward animals.

They came together to form the Society for the Prevention of Cruelty to Animals (SPCA) in London, England, in the 1820s. The formation of the American Society for the Prevention of Cruelty to Animals (ASPCA) followed in New York in 1866. The goal of these organizations was to bring attention to the suffering of animals at the hands of people. By the late 1800s, several other organizations were founded in the United States

The SPCA was formed in London in the 1820s. It later added the word "royal" to its name, so today it is known as the RSPCA. This distinguishes it from the ASPCA, whose early New York headquarters are shown here.

to campaign against animal cruelty. These groups helped create some of the first anti-cruelty laws designed to protect animals from harsh treatment and neglect.

One of the first of these laws was passed in New York in 1867. The provisions of the law were important because they demonstrated that although animals were legal property, they must be treated with concern and cared for under humane guidelines. The law created penalties for abusing animals, keeping animals for fighting, and transporting animals in a cruel manner. This law was also the first to address the abandoning of old or sick animals, as it was common practice when a work animal reached a certain point of age, exhaustion, or disease for it to simply be abandoned in the streets. This provision of the law provided a three-hour window in which an owner could leave an animal on the street—for instance, if someone was shopping and could not take their dog inside the store. Outside of that window, the owner would be charged with abandoning the animal, which was a misdemeanor offense. Within a few years, similar laws were enacted in many other states.

Current laws vary among states. Most address meeting an animal's basic needs by providing food, water, shelter, and medical attention. Others cover specialized topics such as prohibiting the use of chicks and rabbits as contest prizes (California), regulating the confinement of pregnant pigs (Florida), and requiring that dogs be fitted with collars bearing identification tags (Rhode Island). Many laws now also govern the hunting or harassment of wild animals, with quotas and hunting seasons for individual species being established.

WHY DO DIFFERENCES MATTER?

"Maybe it is easier to harm other animals if we distance ourselves from them—we are so different from other animals, we tell ourselves, that it is all right to harm them."

—Marc Bekoff, professor and author of many books on animal behavior and emotions

Marc Bekoff, *Strolling with Our Kin*, Jenkintown, PA: Anti-Vivisection Society, 2000, p. 15.

The Difference Between Welfare and Rights

Animal welfare laws aim to eliminate the unnecessary suffering of animals that are used for purposes considered necessary to people. Generally, these purposes are evaluated based on the benefit they provide people. If human interests can be served through the use of an animal, then that purpose is considered necessary. For example, it is generally considered acceptable to kill animals for food or use them for medical research because those purposes benefit people. Animal welfare laws ensure that animals used in this manner are provided with the best lives possible, given their circumstances. People concerned with animal welfare agree that animals should not be made to suffer unnecessarily to benefit people.

Animal welfare is not the same thing as animal rights. People who work on animal welfare issues use science to determine ways to humanely care for animals. Animal welfare is harm reduction, specifically meant to reduce the unnecessary suffering of animals as much as possible while still making no changes in what people use them for. The animal rights movement, however, is based on an overall belief system. Supporters of animal rights oppose the idea of measuring the value of an animal's life in terms of its benefit to people. This mindset, they believe, reinforces the idea that animals are simply property. Instead of focusing on how people treat animals when they use them, some people feel the real question should be whether the use of animals by people can be justified at all. Trying to balance human interests with those of animals is unrealistic, they believe, because human interests will always win out. Gary Francione, a noted professor of animal rights law, explained,

> *The human property interest will almost always prevail. The animal in question is always a "pet" or a "laboratory" animal, or a "game" animal, or a "food" animal, or a "rodeo" animal, or some other form of animal property that exists solely for our use and has no value except as a means to our ends. There is really no choice to be made between the human and the animal interest*

because the choice has already been predetermined by the property status of the animal.[4]

Some animal rights supporters believe using chickens for egg-laying violates their right to not be used as a resource.

For this reason, Francione advocates a whole new way of looking at animals. Instead of considering them as property owned by people—as is the case in virtually all societies—he believes in applying "the principle of equal consideration." This principle proposes that the interests of animals should count as much as the interests of people. This does not mean that animals should have all the same rights as people; for instance, animals would have no use for the right to vote or the right to own property. This principle is much simpler than that. To Francione, equal consideration means that "we must extend to animals the one basic right that we extend to all human beings: the right not to be treated as things."[5] Using this principle, instead of applying animal welfare laws to govern the size of the cages used to house egg-laying chickens, an animal rights supporter would propose getting rid of chicken farms entirely, because using chickens for egg-laying violates their right not to be used as a resource for humans. Most animal rights supporters believe that it is never necessary to harm or kill animals to benefit people.

Why Are Animals Different?

The idea that animals deserve the same considerations as people gained a growing following in the 1970s, leading to the birth of the modern animal rights movement. At that time, people began to question why animals have always been considered inferior to humans. To answer this question, they looked for qualities that separate people and animals. One quality they considered was the use of language. While the majority of animals do not use human language, scientific studies have discovered that many animals do use complex languages for communicating with others of their kind. Additionally, parrots and corvids—a group of birds that includes ravens and crows—are able to form human words, and they sometimes use these words to communicate with humans, although there is debate about whether they understand what they are saying or just making noises that get a reaction from the humans around them. Several apes have also demonstrated the ability to use American Sign Language (ASL) to carry on conversations with their trainers. Some say this is a clear indication that they can communicate, while others believe the apes are simply copying their trainers' movements in order to receive treats.

AN UNEQUAL RELATIONSHIP

"Animals, whom we have made our slaves, we do not like to consider our equal."

–Charles Darwin, noted English naturalist who described the process of evolution

Quoted in James Serpell, *In the Company of Animals*. New York, NY: Basil Blackwell, 1986, p. 150.

Another area in which humans were once thought to be superior to animals was in the use of tools. However, this has long since been debunked as well. It is now common knowledge that many animals use and even have the ability to make tools.

One argument often made to separate people from animals is that people have greater intelligence and the ability

The Great Ape Project of 1993

The great apes–gorillas, chimpanzees, bonobos, and orangutans–share a close genetic relationship with humans. They also demonstrate many humanlike traits, such as distinct personalities, a high degree of intelligence, and the ability to form strong emotional attachments. Several apes have demonstrated their ability to think and carry on a conversation when they have been taught American Sign Language (ASL). These characteristics inspire many people to have strong feelings of kinship with apes and express concern over the way apes are exploited by people. To protect great apes from use in medical research, the entertainment industry, or other activities that benefit humans, a group of animal rights activists founded the Great Ape Project in 1993.

The controversial goal of the Great Ape Project is to have the United Nations (UN) declare that these animals are granted the same basic rights as humans: the right to life, the right to individual liberty, and the prohibition of torture. This designation would mean that apes could no longer be viewed as property that could be owned and used for human benefit. Critics of the Great Ape Project's goal argue that shared deoxyribonucleic acid (DNA) is not enough to grant human rights to apes. Without a moral sense of right and wrong to drive responsible behavior, they say, apes are not deserving of the same rights as people. The real goal, many people argue, should be minimizing the suffering of apes simply because they suffer, not because they are so similar to humans.

to reason. However, long-term studies of animals such as chimpanzees, crows, and elephants have revealed startling insights into the abilities of animals to think in complex ways, including counting, planning for the future, deceiving others, holding grudges, and adjusting their behavior to new situations. This complex behavior makes it difficult to dismiss

It is common knowledge that many animals use tools in much the same way humans do.

the idea that some animals possess intelligence and the ability to reason. Additionally, in many experiments, birds such as ravens have demonstrated better problem-solving skills than human children.

The Ability to Feel Pain

Animal rights supporters argue that the tests of language, tool use, and intelligence fail to provide evidence of great enough differences between animals and people to justify human superiority. Instead of looking for reasons to defend harming animals, they prefer pointing to reasons why animals should be entitled to the same protection from harm as people. Their argument is based on the issue of morality, or the concept of right and wrong. "Humane treatment of animals is first and foremost a moral issue; it concerns how humans *ought* to behave toward animals,"[6] Francione wrote. Although animal rights supporters acknowledge there are clear differences between animals and people, they point out that animals share one overriding similarity with people—the ability to suffer.

The capacity of animals to suffer is the key argument made for granting animals rights. In 1970, Richard Ryder coined the term "speciesism" to describe the practice of hurting others simply because they belong to a different species. Speciesism, Ryder believed, was a form of discrimination on the same level as racism and sexism and was morally wrong. Ryder and other animal rights supporters believe that it is morally wrong to cause an animal to suffer for any reason, even if that animal's suffering would benefit people. To them, the suffering of an animal should be considered the same as human suffering.

How is animal suffering evaluated? Part of the answer lies with an animal's ability to feel pain. At one time, many people thought that animals were unable to think or feel pain like people do. However, scientists now know that biologically, people have much in common with many animals, such as birds and mammals. Because these animals possess similar nervous systems and react in similar ways to human beings to painful stimuli, one might conclude that humans and animals process pain in a similar fashion.

Less is understood about the ways animals such as fish or invertebrates feel pain. For example, it is common practice to put a live lobster in a pot of boiling water to cook it. This is generally considered acceptable for two reasons: first, because lobsters and crabs break down and spoil quickly after death, so cooking them alive is the best way to ensure that they are safe to eat; and second, because most people do not believe that lobsters have the ability to feel pain. In 2018, some scientists stated that lobsters do have a complex enough nervous system to feel pain; others believe there is no evidence to prove this. However, based on the fact that there is a chance they do feel pain, this practice has been abandoned in some places. For instance, in Switzerland and New Zealand, it is illegal to cook a lobster before it has been electrically stunned, making it unconscious when it is put in the water.

HARD TO ACCEPT

"Common sense suggests that the overwhelming majority of Americans—and indeed of the world's population—will never accept the premise that it is wrong to humanely use animals."

—Daniel T. Oliver, author and critic of the animal rights movement

Daniel T. Oliver, *Animal Rights: The Inhumane Crusade*. Bellevue, WA: Merril Press, 1999, p. 132.

Are Animals Self-Aware?

Even if animals do physically feel pain, is their experience the same as human pain? Certainly what is painful to one animal may not necessarily be painful to another. For example, a horse would barely feel a slap that might be deadly to a mouse. When does the feeling of pain become suffering? Can suffering in animals occur without physical pain as it does in humans, such as suffering from fear or anxiety?

For some people, the answers lie in whether or not animals have an awareness of themselves and their place in the world. This awareness is called consciousness. People who oppose granting rights to animals argue that human consciousness far surpasses that of animals. Many people believe that animals are not capable of full consciousness and are not aware that life can end, so they are not able to appreciate their lives the same way humans can. As a result, it is sometimes argued that animals' lives can never equal those of humans, as they have no pull toward a higher purpose and simply exist without setting goals to achieve. According to author Stephen Budiansky,

> *Our ability to have thoughts about our experiences turns emotions into something far greater and sometimes far worse than mere pain ... Sadness, pity, sympathy, condolence, self-pity, [dissatisfaction], woe, heartbreak, distress, worry, apprehension, dejection, grief, wistfulness, pensiveness, mournfulness, brooding, rue, regret, misery, despair—all express shades of the pain of sadness whose full meaning comes only from our ability to reflect on their meaning, not just their feeling ... Consciousness is a wonderful gift and a wonderful curse that, all the evidence suggests, is not in the realm of the sentient experiences of other creatures.*[7]

While it may be impossible to evaluate the degree to which animals are conscious, that question is irrelevant to most animal rights activists. Animal rights activist Marc Bekoff agrees that understanding animal consciousness has value, but he argued that "well-being centers on what animals feel, not what they know."[8] In his view, a cow does not need to understand its purpose in life to experience suffering. "Human self-awareness may be different, but 'different' does not necessarily translate into 'better' in any moral sense,"[9] Francione wrote.

Noted primate expert Jane Goodall is an outspoken advocate for animal rights and has an explanation for why some people hold the view that animals lack any degree of consciousness:

> *It is easier to do unpleasant things to unfeeling objects—to subject them to painful experiments, raise them in intensive factory farms, and hunt, trap, eat, and otherwise exploit them—than it is to do these things to sapient, sentient beings. Fear in a monkey, a dog, or a pig being is probably experienced in much the same way as it is in a human being.*[10]

Essentially, if people believe that animals have self-awareness and are able to think and feel in a way similar to humans, they are forced to confront some very uncomfortable realities in how they have historically treated animals. If they reject this notion, they can continue treating them as lesser life forms without guilt.

THEY ARE AWARE

"Like us, these animals are in the world, aware of the world, and aware of what happens to them. And, like us, what happens to these animals matters to them, whether anyone else cares about this or not."

—Tom Regan, philosopher and supporter of animal rights

Tom Regan, *Empty Cages: Facing the Challenge of Animal Rights*. Lanham, MD: Rowman & Littlefield Publishers, 2004, p. 59.

Animal Rights as a Moral Issue

Many people who are concerned with the welfare of animals say animals can think, feel emotions, and suffer if mistreated. They also believe that animals have basic biological rights, such as the ability to find food, water, and shelter and to reproduce. However, they disagree with the idea that animals have morals and can behave ethically. "Because only humans are capable of moral and ethical behavior, only humans would have moral and ethical rights,"[11] explained former animal sciences professor Leland Shapiro. Nature is often cruel; a lion makes no moral judgment about killing a gazelle, and housecats often toy with their injured prey before killing it. "One cannot assign moral rights to an individual who does not have moral responsibilities,"[12] Shapiro wrote.

In fact, some people consider it immoral to consider animals equal to humans. University of Chicago law professor Richard Epstein stated,

> *We have quite enough difficulty in persuading or coercing human beings to respect the rights of their fellows, so that all can live in peace. By treating animals as our moral equals, we would undermine the liberty and dignity of human beings—making the slaughters of [Adolf] Hitler, [Joseph] Stalin, or Pol Pot seem no worse than the daily activity of preparing cattle for market. That is one kind of moral equivalence we must never allow. Animals are properly property. To misunderstand the rights of animals is to cheapen the rights of human beings.*[13]

Binti Jua, the adult gorilla shown here, once showed humanlike compassion to a boy who fell into her enclosure.

Other thinkers and researchers have argued that animals can, in fact, behave ethically and that they do have their own sets of morals. For example, Bekoff has stated that chimpanzees essentially police themselves, punishing each other for violating social rules.

In addition to punishing each other, there are many examples of animals behaving kindly toward other animals as well as humans:

In one experiment, hungry rhesus monkeys refused to electrically shock their fellow monkeys, even when it meant getting food for themselves. In another study, a female gorilla named Binti Jua rescued an unconscious 3-year-old (human) boy who had fallen into her enclosure at the Brookline Zoo in Illinois, protecting the child from other gorillas and even calling for human help. And when a car hit and injured a dog on a busy Chilean freeway several years ago, its canine compatriot dodged traffic, risking its life to drag the unconscious dog to safety.[14]

A SIMILAR RIGHT TO LIFE

"To avoid speciesism we must allow that beings who are similar in all relevant respects have a similar right to life—and mere membership in our own biological species cannot be a morally relevant criterion for this right."

—Peter Singer, philosopher whose book *Animal Liberation* significantly influenced the formation of the modern animal rights movement

Peter Singer, *Animal Liberation*. New York, NY: New York Review, 1975, p. 19.

The Start of a Movement

Many people are concerned about the treatment of animals. Hundreds of organizations exist around the world to promote animal welfare and animal rights. These organizations hold a wide variety of viewpoints regarding the use and treatment of animals. Traditional humane organizations seek to prevent animal cruelty and to improve basic treatment of animals, especially pets. Other welfare groups advocate improving the lives of animals used in laboratories or raised for food. Neither of these types of organizations are against the general use of animals. These groups are more focused on animal welfare rather than animal rights. The most vocal animal rights organizations present much stronger messages and often use aggressive methods to reach their goals. The largest animal rights group in the world is PETA, with more than 6.5 million members and supporters. PETA's many programs include campaigns against the livestock and fur industries, the use of animals for research, and the use of animals for entertainment.

Many animal rights organizations have goals similar to those stated by activist Tom Regan, who said, "It is not larger, cleaner cages that justice demands … but empty cages; not 'traditional' animal agriculture, but a complete end to all commerce in the flesh of dead animals; not 'more humane' hunting and trapping, but the total eradication of these barbarous practices."[15]

Animal rights organizations have similar goals to each other but can use very different tactics to achieve these goals. Some groups use societally approved, above-board advocacy methods, such as lobbying members of Congress to encourage them to pass animal rights laws. Other groups go to extremes, engaging in secretive, sometimes illegal activities and sabotage to achieve their aims.

PETA campaigns often involve celebrity spokespeople such as rapper Kid Ink, shown here.

Different Goals

There is no real consensus among members of these groups as to what their ultimate goals are. Many people who belong to animal rights groups do not necessarily realize that they are supporting campaigns to totally end the use of animals as human resources. Although many people claim to support animal rights, in reality, most have views supporting animal welfare instead. Many people who express their support for animal rights still wholeheartedly believe that human beings rank above all other species in terms of importance. They may support lab testing on certain animals, as this research can directly benefit humans by ensuring that new medical treatments are safe and effective for people to take, despite the fact that this testing often kills most of the animals that are tested upon. They may believe that farm animals should be kept under conditions that meet certain basic standards but have no problem with eating meat. Most people fall somewhere between true animal rights supporters and people who believe all animals are property, similar to a piece of farm machinery.

The Rise of Animal Rights Law

Law schools throughout the United States are racing to meet the rapidly increasing demand for courses relating to animal rights and animal welfare. In 2000, there were almost none of these courses available, but as of 2018, 167 law schools in the United States and Canada as well as 11 in Australia and New Zealand offer animal law courses. Courses cover a variety of topics ranging from anticruelty laws to pet ownership issues and may eventually give rise to changes in the way the law views animals. For instance, in May 2018, an Oregon horse named Justice became the first animal to be named as a party in a lawsuit against his former abuser. The lawsuit is seeking payment for the expensive medical problems caused by Justice's abuse, which have prevented him from being adopted into a permanent home. According to the Animal Legal Defense Fund, which represented Justice in the lawsuit, "The Oregon legislature and courts have been a leader in recognizing that animals are sentient beings that occupy a unique position in the law."[1]

1. "Groundbreaking Lawsuit Argues Animals Have the Right to Sue Their Abusers in Court," Animal Legal Defense Fund, May 1, 2018. aldf.org/press-room/groundbreaking-lawsuit-argues-animals-right-sue-abusers-court/.

Many people also have ideas about animal rights that are based more on emotion than logic. For example, most people in the United States have no moral opposition toward eating the meat of a cow or chicken but would be horrified if someone offered them cat or dog meat. Many people oppose medical testing on primates, but have no strong feelings one way or the other toward testing on rats or mice. How cute, affectionate, and similar to humans an animal is are things many people do not realize they are taking into account when thinking about which animals deserve rights.

In Ryder's view, "Basically, it boils down to cold logic. If we are going to care about the suffering of other humans, then logically we should care about the suffering of nonhumans."[16]

Farm Animals

When animal rights activists refer to animal use, they are primarily referring to animals that are raised specifically to create food and products such as leather and fur. In the United States, Americans eat more than 200 pounds (90.7 kg) of meat and poultry per capita (per person), leading to the slaughter of approximately 9 billion animals each year. Per PETA statistics, an additional 1 billion animals worldwide per year are killed in the production of leather.

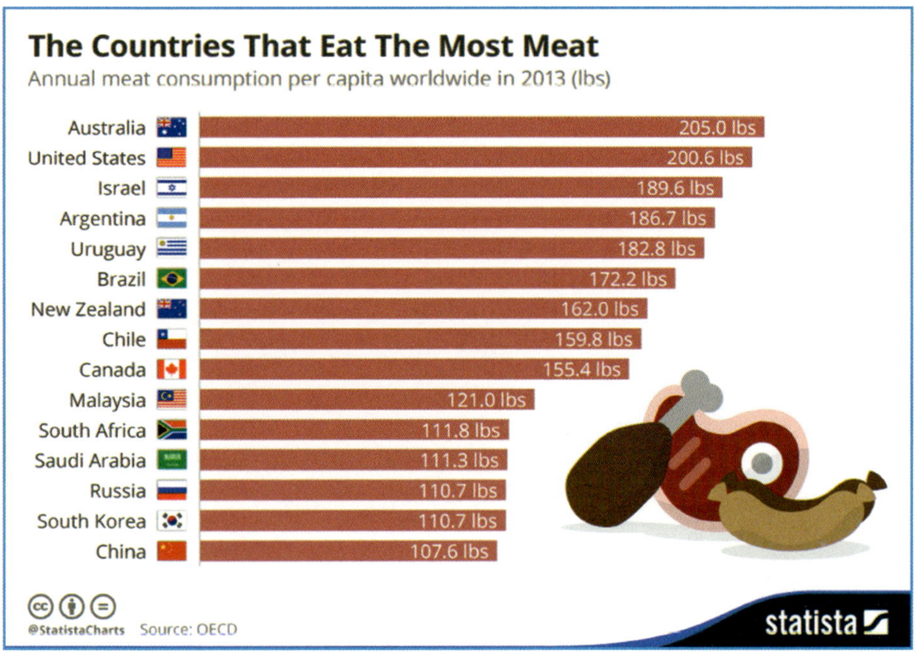

Some countries eat a lot of meat, as this information from the Organisation for Economic Co-operation and Development (OECD) shows. Not only does this impact the animals that are kept and killed to provide this meat, but high meat consumption has also been shown to have negative effects on both the environment and human health.

In order to fulfill the huge demand for meat in the United States while keeping costs down and ensuring that a farm makes money, most food animals are raised on large "factory" farms where thousands of animals are kept in close confinement for their entire lives, often with little space to move freely or behave naturally. Animal rights activists raise many concerns about the treatment and condition of animals raised to satisfy America's demand for meat. People within the agriculture industry respond that consumer demand drives production methods; the more people demand meat, the more animals farms need to raise to satisfy that demand. In some places, this means crowding more and more animals into a limited space. In others, it means cutting down trees to create more farmland; however, this has been shown to have a negative impact on the environment, especially when it is done to raise cattle. Cows produce methane gas, which contributes to climate change. Increasing the number of cows while decreasing the number of trees that can absorb that gas increases global warming.

Confused Morality

Most people give little thought to the process that brings food from the farm to the dinner table. People purchase preprocessed meat in the grocery store in tidy packages that bear little resemblance to the living animal it came from, making it easy for most to ignore the reality of meat production. This tendency troubles critics of the animal agriculture industry who are working to bring more attention to the facts of factory farming.

Animal rights supporters believe that people in developed societies such as the United States, many European countries, and Australia have a double standard in their concern for animals. People in these regions often express great concern for animal welfare, spend large amounts of money on companion animals such as dogs and cats, and voice distress when pets are mistreated. However, most of them shrug off the problems of animals raised for food. It is easy to buy prepackaged pork at the grocery store and not even consider that it was once on a pig. The fact that people do not slaughter their own meat makes it easy to distance themselves from the reality of farming and animal slaughter.

Author and professor Richard Bulliet, an expert in the role of animals in human society, described this trend, writing, "Meat, leather, and test animals are hard to give up, but details about what goes on behind the scenes to provide these goods and cultural services are revolting. Pets and wildlife evoke deep positive feelings, but domestic animals feeding the consumer market are a morally troubling reality."[17]

As an example of this contradiction, James Serpell, author of *In the Company of Animals*, compared society's treatment of traditional pets, such as cats and dogs, and pigs. He described the natural intelligence of pigs, their clean and social nature, and their ability to form strong bonds with people who raise them from piglets. For these reasons, some people do adopt them as pets. In addition, pigs provide people with a wide range of useful products from food to leather—although most people who keep a pig as a pet would not use it this way, which further highlights the difference between an animal that is seen as a beloved pet and one that is seen as a useful tool. In contrast, the millions of cats, dogs, birds, and fish kept as pets provide no real useful purpose beyond companionship. The fact that people get so many commonplace, essential products from pigs makes it easy for many people to ignore the fact that they are intelligent animals—in some cases, much more intelligent than dogs. One

A WORLD OF VEGETARIANS

"I believe a vegetarian world would be a more compassionate world."

–Marc Bekoff, professor and author of many books on animal behavior and emotions

Marc Bekoff, *The Emotional Lives of Animals*. Novato, CA: New World Library, 2007, p. 151.

2015 study found that pigs scored better than dogs and about as well as chimpanzees on basic intelligence tests, such as matching shapes and colors.

Modern Farming

Today, the goal of animal agriculture is to produce the greatest amount of meat at the lowest possible cost. This is, in effect, no different than the goals of any other company: minimize expenses and maximize profit. Animal scientists have increased production through the development of feeds that cause animals to grow more rapidly or produce more eggs or milk. Animals are also selectively bred to create creatures that have leaner meat or other characteristics consumers look for when choosing their meat in stores.

Animal rights activists have long disliked the conditions chickens are kept in.

The main way the industry increases production while keeping costs down is by raising as many animals as possible within a given amount of space. The romanticized idea of animals happily grazing in green pastures on family farms has become a thing of the past for the vast majority of livestock. Modern farms commonly keep animals in very close quarters and extremely confined. This practice makes it easier to maintain animals, which reduces the cost of labor. To keep animals in close confinement, farm managers have to use a variety of practices to maintain the health of their animals.

Animal rights activists condemn many of these animal management practices as cruel and inhumane.

Perhaps the most intensively managed farming involves chickens, raised for both eggs and meat. According to Michael Welch, the former president and CEO of Harrison Poultry, the chicken industry slaughters about 160 million chickens per week to meet consumer demand—a number that has doubled in the last 25 years. In 2015, the HBO show *Last Week Tonight with John Oliver* discussed how chicken farming typically works in the United States. Four large companies—Tyson, Perdue, Sanderson Farms, and Pilgrim's—control the majority of chicken farming. They make contracts with smaller, independent farmers in which the farmers own the equipment needed to raise the chickens and the company owns the chickens themselves. The animals are delivered as young chicks and picked up again about a month later, when they are ready to be killed for their meat. Under these contracts, farmers are required to keep the birds crowded in large, windowless barns. One farmer explained that this is because fresh air and sunlight makes the birds more active. Chickens that do nothing but sit and eat all day get fatter, which means more meat for the companies to sell. Farmers who speak out about the chickens' living conditions are often punished by the large companies by being given chickens that do not sell as well, which hurts the small farmers' profits. This and the equipment the companies require the farmers to buy has put many individual farmers into debt and made them

BETTER FOR CHICKENS AND FARMERS

"I absolutely would do away with solid walls. I would give them back sunlight. Letting sunlight and fresh air in ... number one, the birds love it. And number two, it's better for me."

–Craig, contracted chicken farmer

"Chickens: Last Week Tonight with John Oliver (HBO)," YouTube video, 18:21, posted by LastWeekTonight, May 17, 2015. www.youtube.com/watch?v=X9wHzt6gBgI

afraid to advocate for more humane treatment for the animals. Farmers that do not have contracts with large companies find it hard to compete with them, especially since their product generally costs more due to better treatment of their animals.

Pigs and calves, or young cows, raised in factory farms are also kept in extremely confined conditions. Sows, or adult female pigs, are kept for years in restrictive pregnancy and birthing crates just a little larger than their bodies, which prevent them from being able to turn around. Piglets raised for meat are moved into crowded pens after being neutered. The ends of their canine teeth are cut off, and their tails are removed; both are done to prevent them from biting each another. According to *National Hog Farmer*, "While pain is associated with tail docking, it can be minimized when the procedure is performed as early as possible in a pig's life and with an appropriate analgesia [painkiller]."[18] Shortly after birth, many calves are tied up in stalls, unable to move freely or sometimes even to turn around. They are given no opportunity to exercise and are fed a diet deficient in iron so that their meat will remain pale and tender when they are slaughtered at about three months of age. Meat from these young cows is called veal, as opposed to beef, which comes from adult cows.

The practices used in modern animal agriculture led authors Gaverick Matheny and Kai Chan to make this observation about the quality of life on the farm:

> *These animals have retained instincts from their wild ancestors to explore their environments and develop complex social structures. But in intensive farms, many are confined in static environments, in unnatural group sizes, and exhibit signs of stress and frustration. If these animals' lives are worth living, we suspect they are barely so.*[19]

While they admit some farming procedures could benefit from animal welfare improvements, industry experts say there are many advantages to current practices. They insist that confinement farming allows them to better monitor the animals' health and nutrition, reduces the spread of disease with the use of well-ventilated and sanitary facilities, and provides the animals protection from predators and bad weather. In addition, they claim that these intensive facilities provide animals a less stressful setting for breeding and giving birth compared to animals living in a free-range environment. For example, farmers say that confining sows prevents them from crushing their piglets by accident and reduces sow competition and fighting for food, as would happen if they were allowed to wander freely. "From an animal well-being standpoint, one must compare the benefits of producing cheaper pork, having a lowered mortality of piglets, and fewer injuries to the sows with the confinement housing that is required,"[20] Shapiro stated.

Other people have argued that, while animals in confined factory farming conditions are safer from predators and natural elements, farmers that raise animals in open pasture settings typically have protections in place, such as fences and coops. They say the fact that the animals have no free space and no freedom to wander and graze does not make the painful procedures and cramped conditions of confinement-farmed animals a fair tradeoff.

Slaughtering Livestock

Not all food animals endure the harsh living conditions characterized by factory farming operations. Dairy cattle are generally given room to move more freely within barns and corrals. Beef cattle spend time on both rangelands and more crowded feedlots. However, this does not

Animal rights activists object to the crowded conditions on livestock transport vehicles.

necessarily mean that animal rights activists have no problems or concerns with pasture-farming conditions. There are concerns about the welfare of cattle and other livestock during their transport to slaughterhouses as well as the methods for killing them and processing them into food.

Pigs, sheep, and cattle are transported from farms and feedlots to the slaughterhouse on tightly packed, non-climate controlled transport trucks or railcars. During transport, the animals may be subjected to temperature extremes and lack food and water, often for more than 24 hours. Animal rights groups claim that many animals are injured or die during transport due to trampling, freezing, or dehydration.

Once at the slaughterhouse, animals are supposed to be killed according to the guidelines outlined in the Humane Slaughter Act, a law passed in 1958 to minimize the suffering of animals killed for food. The law requires cattle, hogs, sheep, and horses to be made unconscious by a blow to the head with a stun gun or electric shock prior to slaughter so they are not able to feel pain. However, animal rights organizations claim—and the farming industry acknowledges—that proper stunning does not always take place.

Violation records, videotapes, and interviews with slaughterhouse workers support these claims. "They blink. They make noises … The head moves, the eyes are wide and looking around,"[21] said one slaughterhouse worker who regularly saw animals being processed while they were still conscious. Veterinarian Lester Friedlander, a former government inspector at a hamburger plant, also supported these claims. "In plants all over the United States, this happens on a daily basis," he said. "I've seen it happen. And I've talked to other veterinarians. They feel it's out of control."[22]

One reason slaughterhouses give for why they violate the Humane Slaughter Act is the rate at which animals are processed. In some factories, more than 300 animals go down the production line each hour. At these large factories, cattle are stunned and hoisted onto an overhead chain within 12 seconds of entering the killing chamber. This rate provides workers little time to accurately stun the animals,

Farm-to-Table Restaurants

As more people have become concerned about animal welfare in the 21st century, farm-to-table restaurants have grown in popularity. These are restaurants that commit to serving only locally produced, ethically sourced food. They work directly with farmers, ranchers, and fishers to ensure that the practices of the facility are humane and that the animals are all raised and slaughtered in the immediate area. They also follow quotas set by the government to prevent overfishing. All of this means the menu at a farm-to-table restaurant can be unpredictable. According to *Thrillist* magazine, "For example, in Texas, your daily limit of flounder from the Gulf is 30 fish daily, except in November when your daily limit is two ... All this means is that even if you do have access to seafood that meets your criteria, there just might not be enough of it to put on a menu."[1]

Some people do not like the fact that they cannot rely on their favorite meal to always be on the menu. There might not be enough to go around one day, or something might be out of season in that area. Additionally, food in this type of restaurant is generally much more expensive than at a traditional restaurant that gets its meat from large suppliers. However, this is because the quality of the food is better and the farms are raising fewer animals to give them more space while they are alive. Many people like farm-to-table restaurants because they are better for the environment; for the animals that are raised for their meat; and for people's health, since the food is guaranteed to be fresh and contain no antibiotics or artificial hormones.

1. Emma Diab, "What It Really Means When a Restaurant Is 'Farm-to-Table,'" *Thrillist*, March 24, 2016. www.thrillist.com/eat/nation/what-it-really-means-when-a-restaurant-is-farm-to-table.

forcing them to send the animals down the line even if they are still conscious. If the initial stunning attempt does not properly render the animal unconscious, there is no time to make another attempt before the next animal comes down the line, so they need to keep moving.

Animal science experts who work in the meat industry continue to seek ways to improve the slaughtering process in an effort to enhance animal welfare and slaughter the animals as humanely as possible. Dr. Temple Grandin, an animal sciences professor at Colorado State University, advises slaughterhouses on ways to design facilities and handle animals that would minimize fear and ensure that animals are killed humanely. She also points out that humane slaughter is much more likely when meat buyers monitor the factories. Some food companies conduct audits of factories and will not buy meat from facilities where abuses are recorded. Grandin noted, "Audits by restaurant companies have brought about big improvements in the handling and stunning of cattle and pigs. One of the most effective ways to improve animal welfare in slaughter plants is for large corporations to use their buying power to improve conditions."[23]

Cutting Out Meat

No matter how comfortably animals are raised prior to being slaughtered and how relatively humanely the animals are killed, most animal rights activists do not support the farming and killing of animals at all. Most argue against any use of animals for human benefit, including food, and urge people to adopt a vegetarian or vegan lifestyle. Although meat and dairy products have nutritional benefits, supporters of a vegetarian diet argue that these benefits are overstated and that people do not require meat in a healthy diet as long as they make sure to get the nutrients in meat from other sources. A well-managed, plant-based diet can provide all the nutrients essential for life. In fact, much evidence suggests that plant-based diets are healthier than diets that include a lot of meat—especially red meat such as beef or lamb—which are often linked to obesity, heart disease, and cancer.

Many meat eaters acknowledge the health benefits of being a vegetarian and understand that farm animals often have less than ideal living conditions, which are made worse by people buying and consuming meat. However, some people hesitate to adopt a vegetarian diet because they believe it is inconvenient or that it costs more than a meat-eating diet. Additionally, it can be more difficult to get protein and nutrients found in meat from other sources. If a vegetarian diet is not properly balanced, doctors say, it is no healthier than a diet that includes meat. In addition, many people simply enjoy meat too much to give it up. According to some people, this attitude is morally unacceptable. Francione wrote,

> *Regrettably for those who like to eat meat, this is no argument, and a taste for meat in no way justifies the violation of a moral principle. Our conduct merely demonstrates that despite what we say about the moral significance of animal interests, we are willing to ignore those interests whenever we benefit from doing so—even when the benefit is nothing more than our pleasure or convenience.*[24]

Vegetarians argue that a plant-based diet, in addition to being less cruel than a diet including meat, is also healthier. Vegans take this idea one step further by refusing to eat any products that come from animals, including eggs, milk, and honey.

Others take a more lenient attitude, encouraging people to eat meatless meals at least once a week. Even a small reduction in meat consumption can dramatically reduce the demand businesses must meet, which means they would need to keep fewer animals. Additionally, to make transitioning to a vegetarian diet easier for people who enjoy meat, some companies are experimenting with making plant-based food taste, look, and smell like meat. The Impossible Burger, for instance, is made from potatoes, wheat, coconut oil, and other plants. However, the addition of a molecule called heme makes it taste like a beef burger.

CHAPTER 3

Animals as Test Subjects

Even more controversial than using animals for food is the practice of using them for scientific and medical experimentation. Typically, in medical studies, experimental medications are tested on animals long before they are ever tested on a human being. Most research animals are mice, rats, birds, and fish that are specifically bred for this purpose. Altogether, about 25 million of these animals are used in American laboratories each year. Worldwide, the number is between 60 million and 115 million.

People who argue in favor of animal testing believe that it plays a critical role in the advancement of life-saving medication and treatments for humans. People who argue against it believe it is cruel and say there are other ways to test medication that do not involve subjecting animals to experimental treatments. Through the activism of various animal rights organizations, the use of animal testing has decreased by 50 percent since the 1970s, although many scientists and doctors still believe that it is a critical, useful practice and that using animals for testing greatly decreases the risk of medications and treatments causing unknown effects on people.

Biology and Behavior in Animals

Everyone living today has benefited from the use of live animals in scientific study. Countless medicines, vaccines, surgical procedures, diagnostic tests, and other medical treatments were either discovered or tested through experiments with animals. Since animals became commonly used in research in the early 1900s, advances in medicine have helped increased the human life span by 60 percent, from an average of 47 years to 79 years

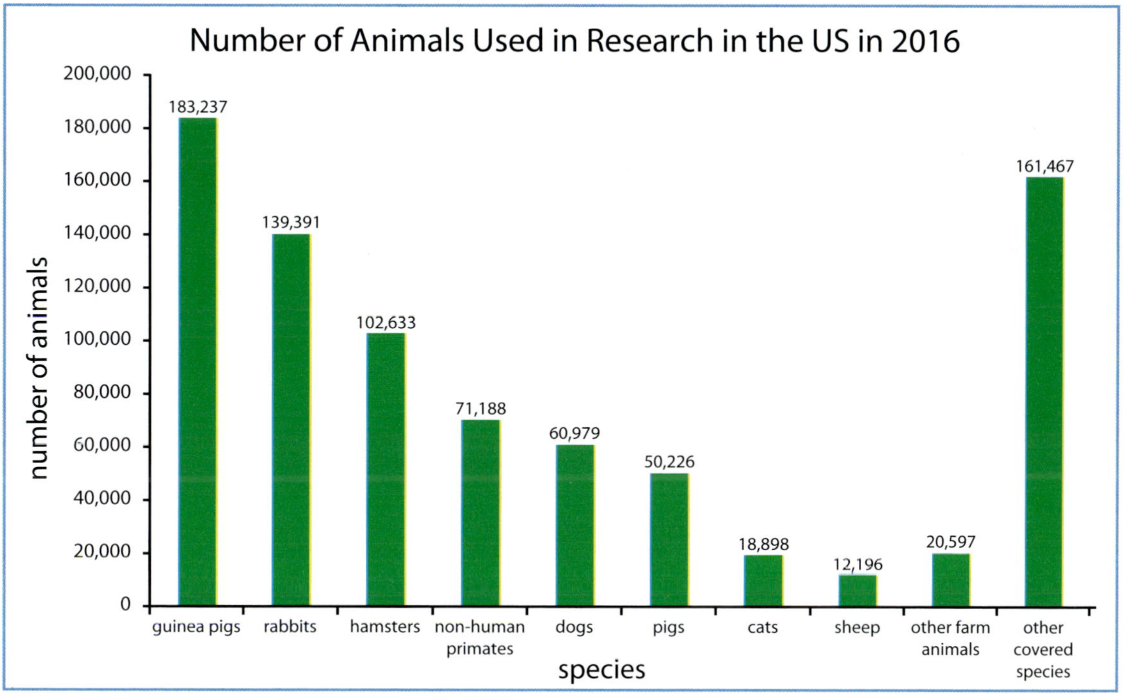

This chart, based on information from the United States Department of Agriculture (USDA), shows how many animals aside from rats, mice, birds, and fish were used for research purposes in 2016.

as of 2018. Two-thirds of the Nobel Prizes awarded in medicine or physiology in the 20th century were given to scientists who used animal subjects in their research. Some of the most notable advances resulting from animal research include vaccines for infectious diseases such as polio and rabies, antibiotics such as penicillin, and medical procedures such as open-heart surgery and X-rays.

Animals are used in research for several purposes. One is to research behavior. By studying what factors influence the way creatures behave, researchers have made many significant advances in the treatment of conditions such as drug and alcohol addiction and mental illness. Behavioral studies on cats resulted in discoveries that led to the development of treatments for strokes and brain damage. Behavioral research is also helping scientists better understand the connection between the body and mind, which can influence diseases such as those relating to stress.

Mice and rats are the most commonly used test subjects because these animals' genetic, biological, and behavioral characteristics are very close to those of humans.

In addition to using behavior in animals to understand human behavior, scientists also study animals' bodies, because, while they are different from human bodies, they still have complex systems that react similarly to various stimuli and diseases. In order for their studies to be as useful as possible, researchers seek out the best animal model for each experiment. Sometimes animals are selected for a study because the animals suffer from the same diseases as humans. For example, rabbits are an important part of studies on the eye disease glaucoma.

STATISTICS ON PAIN

"In 58 percent of all animal research, the animals are not subjected to any pain. In 35 percent ... the animals may have some pain or discomfort and are given pain-killing medication or anesthetics. In the remaining 7 percent of experiments, the animals experience pain, usually because the experiment is studying pain or because anesthesia would interfere with the test results."

–Michigan Society for Medical Research

"Facts and Myths About Animal Research," Michigan Society for Medical Research, accessed on May 2, 2018. mismr.org/facts-myths-about-animal-research/

Growing Opposition to Animal Testing

Despite the reduction in animal testing since the 1970s, animal rights activists believe that all animal testing should be ended immediately. They believe scientists and researchers must find a better way to test medication and research diseases because, they say, the animals are suffering due to their confinement in cages and the painful testing and experimentation the animals are subjected to. They also cite instances of abuse and neglect that they say are the result of cruel and careless researchers. Activists are especially opposed to experiments involving surgery on living animals, a practice known as vivisection.

Opponents of animal experimentation argue that many diseases afflicting people—such as cancer, heart disease, and diabetes—are strongly linked to lifestyle choices such as diet and exercise. Therefore, they insist, scientists should put a greater focus on preventative care and education instead of treatment after the disease has developed. They also believe that using animals in research has limited value for improving human health. Animals typically have a much shorter life span and, although they have complex body systems, they are much different than the systems found in human bodies. This makes it difficult to predict how a disease in a rat might behave when found in a human. Advances in human life span and the decline of killer disease outbreaks are more a result of improved sanitation and better diet than treatments developed through animal studies, they argue.

One of the most controversial tests performed on animals is known as the LD50 test, used to measure the toxicity of drugs or other chemicals, such as household cleaning products. The letters stand for "lethal dose;" the test is used to determine what amount of a substance will kill 50 percent of the test population within a certain period of time. In this test, animals are given a dose of a substance by force-feeding, through injection, or by application to the skin and observed for signs of toxicity. Researchers use the results of this test to determine what dosage of the chemical would be harmful to humans.

Because large numbers of animals die painfully as a result of a single test, the LD50 test has been widely criticized for being cruel. In addition, many people question the accuracy of the test. Results vary widely among species and are affected by the age and gender of test subjects, the dosing technique, and conditions in the lab. These variations lead many to doubt the test's ability to predict a human's reaction to the substance. Due to these concerns, the LD50 test has been banned in the United Kingdom, and its use is on the decline elsewhere. Other tests called the fixed-dose procedure and the up-and-down method are frequently used instead. These tests use a smaller number of animals to find a dose that causes signs of toxicity, but not death. Scientists use the results to calculate the dosage that would be lethal. Multiple nonanimal methods have also been in development since the 1990s.

ANIMAL TESTING: A NECESSARY EVIL?

"When you start with a necessary evil, and then over time the necessity passes away, what's left?"

–Matthew Scully, author and supporter of animal rights

Matthew Scully, *Dominion*. New York, NY: St. Martin's, 2002, p. 386.

Animals as Human Replacements

Animal rights supporters criticize the use of animals to test drugs or product safety. They say animals are poor models for the development of medical treatments for humans, citing cases in which animals respond to diseases and medicines differently than humans do. What works for an animal may not necessarily work for a human being. For example, research showed penicillin to be deadly to hamsters and guinea pigs, but penicillin has been an immensely important drug in human medicine over the years. In contrast, other tests show that some chemicals that are

Cosmetic Testing

In the past, it was common for companies to use animals to test products such as makeup and shampoo to see if they would irritate the skin or eyes. One of the most controversial tests used for this purpose is the Draize test, named after a scientist working for the U.S. Food and Drug Administration (FDA) in the 1940s. The Draize test involves putting chemicals in the eyes of rabbits to determine whether or not a product will irritate or harm the eyes. Rabbits in the test are restrained so they cannot move their heads. The substance being tested is applied to the rabbits' eyes, and then researchers observe the effects, designating a score corresponding to the amount of irritation.

Animal rights groups vocally criticized such research as cruel, which led to public outcry against the test. As a result, many cosmetic companies in the United States have abandoned the practice of testing their products on animals, and it has been banned completely in the European Union (EU). Instead, these companies use ingredients already proven safe in previous animal tests or use human volunteers in their product testing. Some are also using technologically advanced methods such as 3D models made from human skin cells. These companies often use the fact that they do not test on animals as a marketing tool. Their products generally have labels identifying them as "cruelty-free" or "not tested on animals." However, cosmetic testing still happens in some places. The most notable is China, which, according to *Allure* magazine, requires almost all cosmetics to be tested on animals before being sold to humans.

The "cruelty-free" label is a marketing tool used by companies to indicate that the product was not tested on animals.

dangerous to people have little impact on animal health. For example, when exposed to cigarette smoke, dogs and monkeys failed to develop lung cancer the way humans do. When testing a treatment or drug on an animal, scientists need to take all of these factors into consideration. The release of a life-saving drug or treatment may be delayed because it does not work effectively on an animal. Conversely, warnings on health hazards may be delayed as well, as something that is not harmful to an animal may be deadly to a human, due to the vast differences in human and animal physiologies. Veterinarian Jean Greek and her husband, Ray Greek, a doctor, are outspoken critics of the usefulness of animals in medical research. They have analyzed the role of animals in medical advancements and believe that applying results from animal studies to humans is difficult and even dangerous:

> *We were finding, through scientific research, that extrapolating data from animals to humans is either* misleading, unnecessary, dangerous, *or all three …Since we are all putting our lives and the lives of our loved ones in the hands of supposedly rigorous science, is not a model that requires so much fudging grossly inadequate—especially since humans themselves provide the perfect model?*[25]

Although humans are the perfect model for testing the effects of drugs and other medical treatments, safety concerns mean that people are generally used only during the final stages of testing, after researchers already have a pretty good idea of how the drugs work. After conducting rigorous tests called preclinical trials on animals in the lab, researchers perform tests on human patients during clinical trials. These trials determine the proper amounts and best ways to administer the drug or treatment. Often, drugs never advance beyond these trials because they are not effective enough or cause undesirable side effects. Supporters of preclinical trials argue that using people to test potentially dangerous chemicals or drugs suspected of causing birth defects without examining the effects on animals beforehand could cause irreversible damage to the human subjects.

Animals for Education

In addition to their role as subjects for developing medical treatments or testing products, animals are also commonly used for educational purposes. Many animals, including worms, frogs, and pigs, are frequently used as dissection subjects to teach biology to students in classrooms from elementary school to college. Although these animals are already dead when they reach the classroom, they were killed specifically for the lesson. Living animals are also frequently used for educational training purposes, such as providing doctors and veterinarians with opportunities to practice surgery and other procedures.

The role of animals in education is becoming increasingly controversial. Animal rights activists argue that the differences in biology between animals and humans make for limited effectiveness. They argue that performing heart surgery on a pig does not adequately prepare a doctor to perform heart surgery on a person. Instead, they support the use of donated human corpses as well as realistic computer simulations, which provide a much more accurate model of the human heart. Technologically advanced robots called human-patient simulators have also been developed. These models appear to breathe, bleed, and even die if the student makes a mistake. According to PETA, as of 2018, 97 percent of American medical schools have moved to nonanimal training methods.

Research on Primates

The most frequently criticized form of animal research is the use of nonhuman primates—monkeys and apes such as chimpanzees—as test subjects. Because primates are so similar to people, they serve as models for researchers to study many human diseases, such as acquired immunodeficiency syndrome (AIDS), hepatitis, osteoporosis, heart disease, Parkinson's disease, and drug addiction. The similarities between primates and humans also make primates good subjects for studying biological processes such as reproduction and aging. In addition, their intelligence and social systems make primates ideal candidates for the study of language, learning, memory, and other skills requiring complex thinking or social interaction.

The same qualities that make primates such good models for humans, however, also suggest that they experience suffering in much the same way that humans do. Animal rights activists insist that using primates for research subjects them to extreme suffering due to pain and isolation in small cages. Many of the approximately 70,000 primates used in research in the United States are housed in national primate research centers funded by the federal government for research to benefit human health. Some of the primates in these centers are maintained in large enclosures providing natural social groupings, and others are kept as individuals or small groups in more confining cages.

Some primate research is relatively harmless to the animals—researchers simply observe their behavior without causing any physical injury. Other research is more invasive, however, and involves surgery, restraint, and other procedures that can cause pain and anxiety. Some primates are kept in labs and used for many different studies over the course of several years or even decades. Other studies require that the animals be put to death at the end of the test so that their organs and tissues can be examined.

The similarities between primates and humans make primates good test subjects, but many people feel this is unethical.

Vice News interviewed both supporters and opponents of primate testing and found that "everyone agrees that testing on animals is deeply unpleasant, that it would be better if animals were not used, and that phasing out the use of animals in medical research is the ultimate goal. What the animal rights advocates and the scientists disagree on is how much benefit medical testing has brought, how fast animals should be phased out, and how they should be treated in the meantime."[26]

The CHIMP Act

In 2000, President Bill Clinton signed the Chimpanzee Health Improvement, Maintenance, and Protection (CHIMP) Act into law. This law acknowledged that the United States has a moral responsibility to provide lifetime care for chimpanzees used in medical research that is conducted or supported by the federal government. The CHIMP Act provides federal funding for the creation of sanctuaries for housing chimps no longer needed for research purposes.

The first sanctuary established as a result of the CHIMP Act was Louisiana's Chimp Haven. Chimps once used in research by the National Institutes of Health (NIH) have found a new life in retirement at this nonprofit sanctuary supported by both federal funds and private donations. Chimp Haven's setting on 200 acres (81 ha) in the warm countryside provides a more natural life for the chimps, some of which had been taken from the wild before living for decades in a laboratory.

Unfortunately, the CHIMP Act originally placed a limit on the amount of federal funding the NIH could use for the sanctuary. This meant the organization could not afford to place all the former research animals there. To address this issue, in 2013, amendments to the bill were passed that gave the NIH more flexibility in how it could use its funds. As a result, the NIH was able to retire about 90 percent of its chimps.

Humane Research Standards

Most researchers have concern for the welfare of their subjects and go to great lengths to provide the most humane care possible. The use of animals in medical research is regulated by the provisions of the Animal Welfare Act (AWA), a law passed in 1966 to provide minimum standards of care and treatment for certain laboratory animals, including dogs, cats, and primates. The AWA dictates the minimum allowable cage space, as well as standards for feeding, exercise, and social groupings of animals. Research facilities are also required to have an Institutional Animal Care and Use Committee (IACUC) to oversee research activities. The IACUC reviews and monitors the studies to ensure that the use of animals is both necessary and humane.

Despite its significant role in addressing the humane treatment of laboratory animals, the AWA does not go nearly far enough, according to critics of animal testing. Just as the Humane Slaughter Act does not apply to chickens and turkeys—even though they make up 95 percent of all slaughtered animals in the United States—AWA regulations do not cover the care and use of birds, mice, rats, or fish, which represent about 90 percent of all animals used in research. It also does not apply to farm animals that are used for agricultural research. In addition, due to poor funding, there is a limited number of inspectors available to monitor labs with the frequency necessary to be sure they comply with the law. IACUCs, too, are criticized for sometimes not setting strict enough standards for approving research proposals. Because many studies bring significant grant funding to the research facility, IACUCs may approve proposals that have little scientific merit in the interest of obtaining grant money. Opponents of animal testing argue that allowing research facilities to self-regulate does not provide enough oversight, as they will still be largely motivated by self-interest to report that their labs are following the law.

Although they do not always agree with claims that animals in labs are mistreated and suffer, researchers do share some of the concerns of those who oppose animal testing. To demonstrate that the scientific community has genuine concern for the treatment of their laboratory animals, they follow a set of guiding principles known as the Three Rs (reduce, refine, and replace). The Three Rs recognize that the use of animals in research to benefit humans is necessary but can be done in a way that is both scientifically and ethically valid.

Reduce means to limit the number of animals required for an experiment. Selecting the number of animals for a study is a precise science; too few and the results will not be statistically valid, more than necessary and the lives of animals will be wasted needlessly.

Refine means to design experiments in ways that minimize the amount of suffering for the animals involved. If the research is painful, animals must be given anesthesia or painkillers. If the study involves a painful or fatal disease, animals may be euthanized, or put to death, when symptoms begin instead of waiting for the animal to suffer a long and painful death. Refinement also includes improving the quality of everyday life for lab animals by providing nesting materials, toys, and interesting food items.

Replace means that, whenever possible, experiments should be conducted without using animals at all. However, while there have been many successes in finding new ways to conduct experiments that eliminate the need for animals, progress in this area is slow.

Opponents of animal research do not believe the first two practices go far enough to address concerns regarding animal research. They argue that it is unacceptable to kill animals when they develop symptoms of diseases that they were deliberately exposed to, even if it is done to prevent their suffering. They also say that no animals need to die in the name of medical science, so simply reducing the number of animals that die is still a half measure.

WHAT IF IT WERE YOUR DOG?

"When it comes to the sometimes unconscious double standard that people frequently have in the treatment of animals, I find the question 'Would you do it to your dog?' to be a great leveler. If you wouldn't do something to your dog, why would you do it to any other being?"

–Marc Bekoff, professor and author of many books on animal behavior and emotions

Marc Bekoff, *The Emotional Lives of Animals*. Novato, CA: New World Library, 2007, p. 22.

Alternative Research Options

The ethics of using animals in research is a driving force behind the search for alternatives, but it is not the only one. Animal research is time consuming, expensive, and not always accurate, so research facilities are eager to find other ways to develop new drugs or test the toxicity of chemicals. One advancement is the ability of researchers to grow both animal and human cell and tissue cultures in the laboratory. These living cultures are used to study the effects of drugs in treating cancer, AIDS, diabetes, and other diseases.

Powerful computer programs are now available to model disease processes in humans, replacing animal tests for certain studies. Computerized databases also maintain and compile information so tests are not repeated needlessly. In addition, computers are able to identify patterns or trends in diseases that may allow researchers to eliminate more unnecessary, basic studies. Additionally, new procedures have been developed to allow researchers to use human volunteers earlier in the research process without causing them harm. One such procedure is called microdosing. Volunteers are given a tiny dose of a new drug, and researchers monitor how it reacts in their bodies. This can "help screen out drug compounds that won't work in humans so that they won't needlessly advance to government-required animal testing."[27]

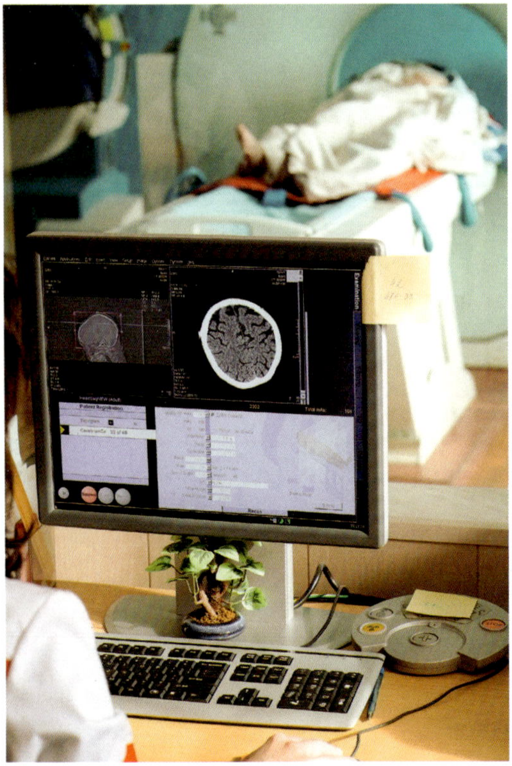

New technologies, such as magnetic resonance imaging (MRI), allow researchers to see inside the bodies of people and animals without harming them, eliminating the need for vivisection.

Most researchers embrace advances that reduce the need for animal testing and understand that their usefulness is limited.

According *NOVA Next*, a science and technology publication associated with the PBS show *NOVA*, 90 percent of new drugs fail:

> *Treatments often seem promising when tested in animals, encouraging pharmaceutical companies to start clinical trials that test safety and efficacy in human patients. But the majority of the time, the investment doesn't pay off. Some are pointing their fingers at animal models, saying they don't accurately represent the human disorder they are designed to mimic. Moreover, their response to treatments doesn't predict a human's response and experiments using them often paint an overly optimistic picture.*[28]

Despite these challenges, some believe that alternatives will never replace the use of animals entirely. So far, at least, these alternatives are unable to completely duplicate the complex biology of living animals. However, as technology continues to advance, new discoveries make this a real possibility in the near future. One promising invention is called organ-on-a-chip. Dr. Donald Ingber put human cells on a microchip in such a way that they behave like real organs. He started with a lung, and it mimics a human lung so well that it has successfully been used to test things such as the toxicity of a cancer drug and the effects of breathing in air pollution. The results the lung-on-a-chip has given in studies are so much more accurate than those that come from animal tests that Ingber and his team have been working on making other organs. According to PETA, "[This] and other non-animal methods are not hindered by species differences that make applying animal test results to humans difficult or impossible, and they usually take less time and money to complete."[29]

With all of these advancements, animal rights activists feel that researchers increasingly have no excuse to continue using animals for research. However, many researchers—even Ingber himself—believe there are certain things, such as the study of behavior, that people will always depend on animal tests for. This will likely continue to be a point of contention for years to come.

Animals as Entertainment

Throughout history, human beings have used animals for sport and entertainment in various ways. Some of these practices are deeply rooted in human culture, dating back to the beginnings of recorded human history. Some celebrate the animals' beauty, strength, and speed. Others harm or kill the animals to entertain people.

Supporters of animal rights are concerned about many of the ways in which animals are used in sports and entertainment. They feel that forcing animals to compete in sports for human benefit is cruel. They claim that these sports promote large-scale suffering of animals as a result of overbreeding, mistreatment, poor veterinary care, and disposal of unwanted animals. Most animal rights activists support ending all uses of animals in sports and entertainment.

People who support the use of animals in sports claim that the animals are simply doing what comes naturally to them, such as running or fighting, with the additional benefit of providing entertainment. They also argue that many uses of animals in sports and entertainment provide cultural benefits and are part of long-standing human traditions.

Animals in Blood Sports

Some of the earliest examples of animals being used for entertainment purposes date back to ancient Rome, Italy. Emperors commonly arranged for wild animals to be captured in Africa and brought to amphitheaters for elaborate shows featuring animal fights and imitation hunts. In front of thousands of cheering spectators, lions, leopards, elephants, crocodiles, giraffes, hippos, and rhinoceroses would fight one another or fight and often be killed by Roman gladiators. On special occasions honoring an emperor's inauguration or achievements in battle, thousands of wild animals were killed over several weeks of festivities. These wasteful displays of animals from exotic locations were used to signify the wealth and power of the reigning leader.

In ancient Rome, large animals were often killed by gladiators in front of cheering crowds.

These often brutal acts of entertainment involving animals were not just limited to ancient times. As recently as the 1800s, the practices of "bearbaiting" and "bullbaiting" were still popular in England. These events featured a bear or bull chained to a post in the center of a public arena. Trained dogs would attack the animal, eventually killing it. Often, several of the attacking dogs were killed in the process. Due to rising public outcry against such events, in 1835, British Parliament banned the practice with the Cruelty to Animals Act. While bearbaiting no longer takes place, other sports featuring animals fighting or being killed continue. Although outlawed in some regions, these "blood sports" such as dogfighting and bullfighting still occur both in public and in private in many places around the world.

A Spanish Tradition

One of the most controversial sports involving the killing of animals is bullfighting. Although its history is uncertain, the sport may have descended from earlier contests between people and animals in ancient Rome. Today's bullfighting is firmly rooted in Spain, where it has been practiced for

Zoos: Animal Prisons?

Each year, more than 195 million people in North America visit zoos and aquariums accredited by the Association of Zoos and Aquariums. These visits provide opportunities for people to see and learn about wildlife from all over the world through exhibits, classes, and other presentations. Zoos are also active in conservation efforts for many endangered animals. Each year, they spend millions of dollars to study and preserve hundreds of species both in captivity and in their wild habitats.

Many animal rights organizations insist, however, that zoos are little more than collections of caged animals and that they do little to educate the public on wildlife conservation issues. Activists claim that most people visit zoos for entertainment, not education, and that this promotes the idea that humans are better than animals rather than encouraging connection with them. They insist that wildlife education can be better achieved through film documentaries instead of keeping animals in captivity. They also claim that most zoo exhibits are unable to provide environments that encourage animals to behave naturally. As a result, they believe that animals suffer both mentally and physically from being deprived of their freedom. Studies have shown that putting animals in zoos can lead some animals to develop a condition called "zoochosis," which is mental illness caused by being put into zoo habitats that give them much less room than their natural habitats. Additionally, one study published in the journal *Science* found that elephants live much longer in the wild than in zoos.

Zoo supporters argue that zoos provide opportunities for families to connect with animals on a personal basis, fostering feelings of amazement and appreciation of the natural world. These feelings lead people to consider their role in protecting the environment. Many zoos are now studying the ways people learn during their visits. Their discoveries will help zoos design exhibits and programs that are even more valuable for developing environmental awareness and encouraging visitors to participate in conservation efforts.

more than 1,000 years. It is also popular in France, Portugal, Mexico, and some other Latin American countries.

As a bullfight begins, men on horseback spear a bull in the neck and shoulders to weaken and infuriate it. Next, other men move in on foot to thrust barbed sticks into the bull's back to further enrage it. As blood flows from its wounds, the bull charges the matador, who encourages it to attack by waving his cape. The matador is applauded for close brushes with the bull's horns as he dodges the angry animal running by. The closer he dodges, the more skill he is displaying. Finally, as the bull weakens, both from exhaustion and the wounds that were previously inflicted upon it, the matador stabs it between the shoulder blades with his sword to make the kill.

DO ZOOS CHANGE PEOPLE?

"[T]here is no compelling [convincing] or even particularly suggestive evidence for the claim that zoos and aquariums promote attitude change, education, and interest in conservation in their visitors."

–Emory University researchers

Quoted in Laura Smith, "Zoos Drive Animals Crazy," *Slate*, June 20, 2014. www.slate.com/blogs/wild_things/2014/06/20/animal_madness_zoochosis_stereotypic_behavior_and_problems_with_zoos.html.

Supporters of bullfighting praise the matadors' technique and bravery, comparing them to gifted artists. Isabel Carpio, secretary-general of the Union of Fighting Bull Breeders, views the contest as beautiful and believes that a top matador "is like a sculptor who is molding, not clay, but the animal."[30] Many also cite bullfighting's strong historic connection to a region's culture. "It is a cultural component that comes from times that we no longer even remember," said a young Spanish woman attending a bullfight. "It is something that is ours, something intrinsic [essential]. It is a world that once you enter, you like it more and more, and you want to be more a part of it."[31]

In contrast to its supporters, many people view bullfighting as an outdated sport that promotes the torture and suffering of animals. Critics point out that the time in the ring is extremely stressful and painful for the bull, ultimately leading to its death. Estimates vary, but according to the Humane Society International, at least 250,000 bulls are killed in Spain each year during bullfights. Many horses also die in the ring after being gored by enraged bulls. Miguel Moutinho, the leader of a Portuguese animal welfare group, expressed scorn toward matadors. "Bullfighters like to say they are artists but [the bullfighter] is a murderer and bullfighting is an immoral spectacle,"[32] he said.

Both opinion polls and bullring attendance show that support for bullfighting is declining. According to the BBC, the Spanish government reported in 2015 that only 9.5 percent of its people had attended a bullfight that year. Animal rights groups regularly stage protests outside bullfighting arenas and are pressuring the government to ban the practice, although even some people who do not like the sport do not necessarily want it banned. Some simply want it to be made more humane—for instance, by killing the bull quickly with a sword or electric prong instead of making it suffer by stabbing it multiple times. Spain already has strict laws against animal cruelty, but those laws make exceptions for bullfighting. Activists argue that saying something is rooted in culture is no excuse to kill thousands of animals on an annual basis.

Public opinion appears to be turning against the practice even in Spain, where bullfighting is most widespread and has historically been honored in an almost religious way. According to a World Animal Protection poll in 2016, 19 percent of adults in Spain support bullfighting, while 58 percent oppose it. In September 2016, protestors flooded the streets of Madrid to condemn the practice as a national shame in the largest anti-bullfighting demonstration in history. Madrid resident Azucena Perez, a participant in the demonstration, summed up the prevailing sentiment, stating,

Bullfighting has long been a tradition in Spain, but in recent years, public opinion has begun turning against it.

"I think our laws should prohibit the torture of animals as a form of entertainment."[33]

Fighting Dogs

Another blood sport is dogfighting, and it is popular in some parts of the United States. It is illegal in all states to attend a dogfight, even if the person is not directly participating. However, an underground culture of dogfighting has persisted, especially in southern states. Dogfighting is also associated with other types of criminal activity, including gambling, illegal weapons, and drug possession.

Traditional dogfighting is a highly organized activity run by professional breeders who invest a great deal of time and money into staging fights and developing generations of fighting dogs. They get their investment back by charging a lot of money to people who want to see the fight. The most commonly used breeds are the American pit bull terrier, the American Staffordshire terrier, the Staffordshire bull terrier, and the American bully. All of these breeds have similar genes, behaviors, and looks, and all four are often called simply "pit bulls." However, "pit bull" is not a true breed, but rather a description of these four distinct breeds. Pit bulls possess such a strong drive to fight that if they are provoked, they will often fight to the death instead of backing down when injured or overpowered. They are also extremely loyal dogs, which, in addition to their natural tendencies, makes them willing to continue to fight for their masters, even when grievously injured. This association with dogfights has unfortunately given pit bulls a terrible reputation;

many people think they are likely to attack people even when unprovoked. Some communities and housing complexes even ban residents from owning pit bulls, and often, this is enforced based only on what the dog looks like—even when it does not share any genetic similarities with the four breeds previously mentioned. Only recently have people begun to realize that these dogs are not naturally vicious. According to the ASPCA,

> *[Being used for dogfighting] does not mean that the pit bull is unsuitable as a family pet. It is important to remember that any dog can behave aggressively, depending on the context, his genetic background and his upbringing and environment. When a dog is treated well, properly trained and thoroughly socialized during puppyhood and matched with the right kind of owner and household, he's likely to develop into a well-behaved companion and cherished member of the family.*[34]

Rather than being treated as pets, fighting pit bulls undergo extensive training to prepare for fights. They are forced to run on treadmills to build endurance, often with the dangling bait of a cat or rabbit to encourage them to keep going. Their owners also encourage them to be aggressive by doing things such as starving and hurting them. It is common practice for people to train their dogs to fight each other by starving them, then chaining them together and giving them one bone to fight over.

During competitions, pairs of dogs are released into a pit, where they immediately attack one another. Matches end either when one dog is too injured to continue fighting and quits or when one of the dogs is killed. Owners sometimes kill animals that quit by hanging, shooting, or electrocuting them. Top dogs are highly valued for both fighting and breeding purposes.

Most people were unaware that dogfighting was still a problem until 2007, when National Football League (NFL) quarterback Michael Vick pled guilty to involvement in dogfighting and spent 18 months in federal prison. However, instead of discouraging dogfighting, some say Vick's involvement actually made it more popular. "I don't think Vick's arrest or prosecution stopped those who are predisposed to engage with fighting. In fact … some could argue that the lack of accountability and the fact he [later returned to] the NFL showed no real consequences at all,"[35] said Scott Heiser, the head of the criminal justice program at the Animal Legal Defense Fund. Unfortunately, it is difficult for law enforcement to find and stop dogfighting because it is such a well-kept secret. Like making a drug bust, breaking up a dogfighting ring requires undercover infiltration. Additionally, after the people are arrested, the dogs need to be taken care of. Law enforcement officials cannot investigate every dogfight case because they often do not have the resources available to help the dogs.

Supporters of dogfighting defend their sport, saying it is not cruel because the dogs want—and even love—to fight. Pit bull breeder Bill Stewart explained, "It's about two highly conditioned athletes going at each other with everything they have to try to win. It's the purest form of combat on earth."[36]

Opponents of dogfighting disagree with these sentiments, believing that dogs are willing to fight each other to please their masters or to follow their natural survival instincts and pointing to examples of pet pit bulls that have not been raised to fight showing no signs of aggression or desire to fight. They also point out instances of "trunking," which is

MAKING MONEY ON DOGFIGHTS

"The minimum [number of] spectators on a weekly basis is 500 people … They have a casino type of atmosphere. They have roulette wheels, backgammon, dominos. There can be a minimum bet of $5,000 per fight."

–Richard "Kudo" Couto, founder of Animal Recovery Missions (ARM) Investigations, describing professional dogfighting events

Quoted in Christina M. Russo, "Michael Vick May Have Actually Made Dogfighting More Popular," *The Dodo*, January 21, 2016. www.thedodo.com/michael-vick-dogfighting-more-popular-1565236921.html.

a type of dogfight in which two dogs are put into the trunk of the car. The dogfighters drive around town, playing music loudly to cover up the sounds of the fight, and then open the trunk later to see which dog is still alive. Many say this shows that dogfighting is more about money and killing than it is about athleticism.

Rodeo: A Western Tradition

Many people agree that blood sports such as bullfighting and dogfighting promote animal cruelty and should be illegal. However, the cruelty of other legal sports involving animals is the subject of debate. One such sport is rodeo. Rodeo is a sport with origins in the roping and riding skills once commonly used by cowboys. Today, rodeo has become a big business in the United States and Canada, with professional rodeo stars competing for millions of dollars in prize money.

Most fans view rodeo as wholesome family entertainment, but animal rights activists criticize many rodeo events. Critics claim that rodeo animals are subjected to cruel treatment during events such as bronco and bull riding as well as steer wrestling and calf roping. They feel these events subject animals to unnecessary confusion and fear. The Professional Rodeo Cowboys Association (PRCA) strongly disagrees with this claim. The organization says it has a thorough animal welfare policy in place for the treatment of animals in the rodeos it sanctions. It also requires that a veterinarian attend all events. Rodeo organizers stress that it is in their economic interest to treat rodeo stock well. Rodeos contract with livestock owners who make large investments to provide the best performing animals possible. Abused and injured animals would perform poorly and cause their owners to earn less or go out of business entirely. Many bucking horses and bulls perform for years, becoming stars in their own right.

Rodeo opponents dispute that horses and bulls are treated well and point to several practices they believe are cruel. One is the use of flank straps placed around the abdomens of bulls and horses to encourage them to buck. Critics say the straps are painful and cause injury to the animals, which is why the animals are driven to buck. The PRCA counters that flank straps do not cause pain. Instead, they say, the strap simply encourages the animal to kick its legs higher while bucking, resulting in a more dramatic performance by the rider.

Animal rights groups have encouraged people to protest rodeos when they come to town, but public opinion largely does not support this.

The other rodeo event most often criticized is calf roping. In this event, a rider on horseback throws a loop of rope around the neck of a running calf, pulling it to a rapid stop. The sudden jerk of the rope can cause injury to calves, including broken necks, backs, and limbs. To help minimize injuries, PRCA rules prohibit flipping or dragging the calf, but even so, sometimes calves are hurt or killed.

The efforts of animal rights groups to prove rodeo animal abuse and shut down rodeos have so far been largely unsuccessful, as most people do not view it as being outwardly harmful or cruel, and, much like bullfighting in Spain, it is a tradition that goes back many years. PETA representative Amy Rhodes said, "We want rodeo out of business, but we know it's not going to happen overnight."[37]

Controversy Over Horse Racing

Another sport targeted by animal rights activists is horse racing. Thoroughbred horse racing, a multibillion-dollar industry, is the leading animal sport in the United States. For instance, the Kentucky Derby is a highly celebrated race and social event, popular even with people who do not often follow the sport. Occasionally a racehorse becomes a

Animals in Hollywood

Hollywood has a long history of casting animals in movie and television roles. When the practice first began, little concern was given to the welfare of the animal actors. However, when a horse was killed after being ridden over a cliff during the filming of the movie *Jesse James* in 1939, there was great public outcry. As a result, in 1940, animal safety representatives from the American Humane Association (AHA) were given the authority to monitor the welfare of animal actors. Eventually, the group developed a set of guidelines that is now used to safeguard animals used in any sort of filming, including movies, television, commercials, and music videos. Films that comply with all guidelines are awarded the ability to include the phrase "No animals were harmed in the making of this film" during their end credits. However, production companies are still sometimes accused of mistreating animals. For example, in 2012, the producers of *The Hobbit* were accused of ignoring the fact that the horses used in the movie were kept in dangerous conditions that caused up to 27 of the animals' deaths. The production company denied the accusations, stating that as soon as the conditions were brought to its attention, it upgraded the stable facilities to prevent further injuries and deaths. The AHA confirmed that it had examined the site and made suggestions that could improve the horses' safety, which a spokesperson said the company followed.

For this and other reasons, animal rights organizations object to the use of animal actors. They say that many trainers use cruel practices to force animals to perform for the cameras. They are especially critical of the practice of using great apes, such as chimpanzees and orangutans, in the industry. Because of the strength and aggressive nature of these animals, activists claim that heavy-handed training methods are often required. They document many cases of punishment by beating or other cruel treatment. They also claim that many of these social animals are forced to endure solitary lives in small, cramped cages and spend long hours traveling. In addition, animal rights supporters condemn the action of taking these animals from their mothers during infancy in order to provide cute, young animals for filming.

household name after a winning season, gaining the privilege of retiring to a breeding farm. For most horses, however, the racing life is not so glamorous.

Critics of horse racing point out the physical toll that training and racing has on the fragile bodies of these highly bred animals. Horses begin racing at age two when they are not yet fully mature. As a result, horses suffer frequent injuries to their feet and legs. To keep them in competition, trainers and veterinarians may give painkilling drugs to horses with illnesses or injuries.

Massive injuries, such as shattered leg bones, and even deaths are not uncommon during training or races. In fact, hundreds of racehorses die at tracks each year. Horses are often killed upon suffering broken legs. "It's part of the game,"[38] said one jockey, or horse rider.

THE ENTERTAINMENT OF ABUSE

"It's animal abuse merchandised as family entertainment ... This is not family entertainment. How do you think kids feel when they see some little animal get its neck broken?"

—Peggy Larson, veterinarian and former bronco rider, referring to rodeo

Quoted in Claudia Rowe, "Pros and Cons of Rodeo Roping and Riding," *New York Times*, June 16, 2002. www.nytimes.com/2002/06/16/nyregion/pros-and-cons-of-rodeo-roping-and-riding.html.

Due to the great expense of buying, housing, feeding, and training racehorses, owners tend to treat their horses as investments, making decisions about their futures based on their earning potential rather than the animal's welfare. Winning horses can earn millions for their owners through prize money and breeding fees. Losing horses, however, are sold or retired to adoptive owners. Many injured horses are euthanized, or killed, so the owners do not have to spend money on veterinary fees for an animal that has no future earning potential.

Critics point out that horse racing exists primarily to generate money through both legal and illegal gambling. However, there are many people involved in racing who genuinely love and care for horses and admire their beauty and passion for running. Still, some question whether the sport is justified. George Vecsey, a sportswriter for the *New York Times*, wrote, "These fragile thoroughbreds do not exactly have much say, other than demonstrating that they love to run. Perhaps that is why we love them and respect them and protect them, although not nearly enough from the stress of racing itself. After what we put them through, do we love them so much out of guilt?"[39]

Animal Rights in the Wild

While many people argue over whether or not domesticated animals should be used for food, research, and entertainment, there is also controversy regarding how they should be treated in the wild. Hunting wild animals is still a common activity, but it has become increasingly controversial in recent years, especially regarding the reason for hunting. Throughout the past several decades, animal rights groups have mounted a wide variety of campaigns aimed at influencing the public's attitude toward these activities in an effort to bring an end to the practice, which they believe is both cruel and immoral. Some of these efforts seem to be working. While most people still believe it is acceptable to hunt for food, fewer people support hunting for trophies and fur. Big game hunting, in particular, is more unpopular than it has ever been, and fewer people wear fur now than ever before.

The Tradition of Hunting

The viewpoint that there should be limitations on how and why people use wild animals is a relatively recent development. Primitive humans began hunting wild animals more than 1 million years ago, as a necessity for survival. Even after people began relying on agriculture to provide food, hunting was still a very common practice for obtaining meat to eat and gaining hides and fur for making clothing. In a few places, hunting remains the primary method for acquiring food today. This includes Inuit communities in the Arctic, where the climate makes agriculture close to impossible. Many animal rights organizations do not have objections to hunting when it is necessary for providing for the daily needs of people. This type of hunting is called subsistence hunting. Today, however, hunting in the United States is rarely viewed as a necessity and is generally considered a recreational activity. Although many hunters still consume the animals they kill, most participate in the sport for the thrill of the hunt and the opportunity to enjoy time in nature with family and friends. The meat they get from the animals they kill is more of a bonus than the main reason for hunting.

In recent decades, animal rights groups have begun to condemn hunting as a nonessential activity in the modern world. Since there are so many alternate ways to get food, activists claim, there is no functional reason for hunting. "Although it was a crucial part of humans' survival 100,000 years ago, hunting is now nothing more than a violent form of recreation that the vast majority of hunters does not need for subsistence,"[40] PETA claims. Some of the strongest objections to hunting are aimed at practices viewed as particularly unsporting—when animals are given virtually no chance of escape. Some of these activities include the use of high-tech tools to attract and kill animals; baiting bears with food so hiding hunters can shoot them; chasing bears, bobcats, and mountain lions into trees with dogs; and hunting wolves and other predators from helicopters. Hunters already have a huge advantage over their prey, as they are typically armed with guns and most

In the United States alone, hunters kill about 200 million animals each year.

of the animals they are hunting only have the ability to defend themselves by fleeing. Other concerns are the suffering of wounded animals that escape and the impact that the fear and stress of the chase have on the ability of the animals to feed, travel, and rest.

THE HUNTER'S RESPONSIBILITY

"Part of what makes hunting such an intensely emotional experience is the physical responsibility you take for the death of your food."

—Margaret Knox, author

Quoted in James A. Swan, *In Defense of Hunting*. San Francisco, CA: HarperSanFrancisco, 1995, p. 239.

The Conservation of Hunting

Supporters of hunting argue that instead of harming animals, their activities actually help conserve wildlife populations and habitats, as they can help reduce overpopulation. Overpopulation decreases a species's chances of survival because all the members of that species are competing for limited resources. Hunters and biologists say that by hunting a certain percentage of the population, they are giving the remaining animals access to more resources, which ensures their survival. Legally hunted game species are carefully managed by state wildlife agencies that strictly regulate the number of each type of animal killed. Fees from hunting and fishing licenses as well as taxes from ammunition and other hunting products provide financial support for state fish and wildlife management programs. In 2014, the U.S. Fish & Wildlife Service (USFWS) reported that various state agencies received about $200 million from these licenses. Additionally, the 11 percent tax on firearms, ammunition, and archery equipment that was established by the 1937 Federal Aid in Wildlife Restoration Act "is the single biggest source of money collected nationally for wildlife,"[41] according to Montana's hunter's education website. Each year, this tax alone generates about $86 million. Through hunter-supported conservation efforts, populations of many game species that were once in decline have made notable comebacks. For example, in the 1920s, there were 300,000 white-tailed deer, 30,000 wild turkeys, and 50,000 elk in the United States. Now, those populations stand at about 30 million deer, 7 million turkeys, and 1 million elk. In fact, experts say it is now to the point where some of these animals are starting to become overpopulated again, especially since the numbers of their natural predators, such as wolves and bears, have declined. Just as hunting helped them make a comeback, it can also help keep their numbers under control. When deer in particular are overpopulated, they are more likely to have encounters with humans that are dangerous, such as causing car crashes, damaging crops, and transmitting ticks that carry diseases. They also pose a threat to wild plant species by eating too many of them. In the absence of an adequate number of natural predators, controlled hunting is one tool that can keep animal populations at a number that is beneficial for both the species and humans. According to Thomas Rooney, Ph.D., an assistant professor of biological sciences at Wright State University, "Controlled hunts are conducted in small areas—such as a park or municipality—and

Biologists say controlled hunts can help keep deer populations at an appropriate number.

they are usually managed to reduce the number of deer present drastically … Controlled hunts are often very effective in rapidly decreasing deer population sizes, as long as the targeted area is small."[42]

In addition to pointing to their contributions to wildlife conservation, pro-hunting organizations also take the stance that most hunters possess a deep respect and reverence for nature. They are angered by the campaigns of animal rights groups that portray hunters as unfeeling killers who care nothing about wildlife. Most hunters, these organizations insist, have a deep sense of connection and commitment to the land.

Opponents of hunting claim that, if people wanted so badly to contribute to conservation efforts, they could simply donate the money they would spend on a hunting license toward conservation causes. They also tend to be more supportive of nonhunting deer control efforts, such as installing fences and flashing lights to keep deer away from human areas or reintroducing natural predators to the area.

Hunting for Trophies

While many nonhunters do not mind the hunting of animals such as deer and ducks for sport or food, most are horrified by trophy hunting. Trophy hunters pursue the largest, most exotic, and rarest creatures to kill in order to display their mounted bodies or enter their feats in hunting record books. Trophy hunters are generally wealthy individuals who may spend tens of thousands of dollars traveling to remote locations and hiring hunting guides to lead them to their prey, such as polar bears, lions, elephants, zebras, and giraffes.

Animal rights advocates condemn the practice of trophy hunting outright. One former president of the Humane Society said,

> *It's a perverse and destructive subculture. Thousands of animals suffer and die for the amusement of wealthy elites who have the means to pursue any form of recreation, but choose to shoot the world's rarest and most beautiful animals. There's*

Hunting in Decline

Whether a result of anti-hunting campaigns by animal rights advocates or simply a reflection of changing times, participation in hunting has been declining since the middle of the 20th century. A survey released by the USFWS in 2017 showed that participation in hunting has decreased from 14.1 million people in 1991 to 11.5 million people in 2016. In addition, total expenditures by hunters dropped by 29 percent, from $36.3 billion in 2011 to $25.6 billion in 2016. While animal rights groups are happy about this change, it has had an unintended negative effect: a decrease in the amount of money available for animal conservation.

While interest in hunting appears to be fading, that does not mean Americans are not spending time outdoors. According to the same survey, 86 million people participate in some kind of wildlife-related outdoor activity, such as bird-watching and nature photography. Experts are trying to figure out effective ways to get funding from these activities, but it is harder to license a bird-watcher than a hunter.

While interest in hunting appears to be fading, Americans are still spending time outdoors. Nature photography is one popular outdoor pastime.

no societal value to the exercise, just a selfish all-consuming mentality of killing, collecting, and showing off trophies. They know the price of every animal, but the value of none.[43]

Supporters of trophy hunting say that the large sums of money they spend to bag their prizes support conservation by encouraging local people to protect wildlife for its economic value. Some African governments have created limited hunting opportunities, allowing people to shoot even some of their endangered wildlife, in an effort to raise money and boost local employment. As with recreational hunting, opponents argue that if trophy hunters were interested in conservation, they could donate the money they spend on hunting safaris to conservation organizations without killing lions.

One of the strongest advocates of trophy hunting is the organization Safari Club International (SCI). SCI maintains a record book that details hunting statistics of thousands of trophy animals. The organization presents annual awards to members for their most impressive hunting achievements. Former SCI president John J. Jackson III explained his view of trophy hunting: "A trophy of any species attests that its owner has been somewhere and done something, that he has exercised skilled persistence and discrimination in the agile feat of overcoming, outwitting, and reducing game to possession."[44] However, others disagree with this view because of SCI's practice of counting trophies taken on captive hunts. These take place on private, fenced hunting ranches both abroad and in the United States. Because many of the exotic animals living on these ranches have become accustomed to humans and are confined by fences, the degree of difficulty in these hunts is greatly reduced. In the view of the Humane Society, "SCI ignores the concept of 'fair chase' that many traditional hunters believe in."[45]

While they are popular with some hunters willing to pay for a guaranteed trophy, captive hunts are a rare instance of common ground between both animal rights advocates and some members of the hunting community, both of whom are highly critical of the practice. Humans already have a huge advantage in hunting, being armed with guns. Fencing in animals so they cannot escape completely removes any aspect of sport, critics say.

The level of public outrage over trophy hunting became clear in 2015, when a dentist named Walter Palmer paid $50,000 to hunt lions on a private wildlife refuge in Zimbabwe, Africa. He shot and killed a lion named Cecil, not realizing that Cecil had been collared and tracked by researchers and was a favorite of the locals. The news went viral, causing people to post angry messages online that sometimes included threats to Palmer. The public's outrage increased when it became known that lion hunting was not allowed in the area where Cecil had been killed. Palmer apologized and stated that he had relied on the advice of the hunting guide he had hired. However, his reputation was still heavily damaged.

Some animal rights activists called for lions to be outlawed as potential trophies so they would be protected. However, according to Zimbabwe-based ecologist Vernon Booth, this would have the opposite of the intended effect. The *New York Times* reported,

> *Booth … said that lions were now protected because of the high value attached to them as trophies. Locals tolerate them because of the income that trickles down [from fees for captive hunts]. Without the trophy hunt money, locals would increasingly poison lions, which are considered dangerous to people and livestock, he said.*
>
> *"If there is a complete ban on lion hunting, the tolerance levels for lions would just plummet," Mr. Booth said. "And in wild areas outside of the protected areas, lions would be exterminated, and very quickly. Even though hunting may seem unpalatable [unpleasant] to a lot of people around the world, it is actually very, very necessary."*[46]

Conservation experts say far more wild animals are killed in Africa by local residents or by poachers—illegal hunters—than by trophy hunters. This is because there are strict regulations on trophy hunting that poachers ignore.

Trophy hunters are wealthy individuals who spend many thousands of dollars for the opportunity to hunt exotic animals.

Hunting for Fashion

Another controversial use of wildlife as a human resource is the killing of animals to provide fur for the fashion industry. More than 50 million mink, chinchillas, foxes, coyotes, lynx, beavers, and other wild animals are harvested for their fur every year. The majority of fur is produced on fur farms. On these farms, animals are housed in an extremely confined manner similar to factory farms that raise domestic animals for food, and they face many of the same criticisms for this.

Fur is also obtained by trapping animals living in the wild. Trappers use snares, underwater traps, and leg-hold traps to catch their prey. This method of hunting wild animals—especially the use of leg-hold traps—is strongly criticized by animal rights groups because of the high degree of pain and suffering it can cause animals. Animals caught in leg-hold traps generally suffer severe crushing injuries to the trapped limb. In its frantic struggle to free itself, an animal may chew or twist off its own leg. Eventually, the animal becomes exhausted and may die of exposure and shock or may wait

Although fur is still used in fashion, many clothing and fashion designers have adopted a fur-free policy in response to public criticism.

trapped for several days until the trapper returns to kill it. Because leg-hold traps cannot select their targets, they claim many accidental victims, including dogs and cats. Several states and cities have banned the use of leg-hold traps because of safety and humane concerns.

Because of publicity about the conditions animals face on fur farms and the suffering experienced by animals captured in the trapping industry, the wearing of fur is now much less accepted by the public than it was a few decades ago. Many clothing designers and retailers, especially in the United States and the United Kingdom, have adopted a fur-free policy for their products in response to pressure from both their customers and animal rights groups.

However, not everyone has adopted this policy. The website Quartz reported, "Between 2008 and 2013, world fur exports more than doubled, from $2 billion to more than $4 billion, according to data from the International Trade Centre, a joint agency of the United Nations and the World Trade Organization."[47]

Many animal rights activists believe there is no way fur can ever be ethically sourced. Others, however, disagree. Quartz outlined some instances in which businesses might be able to satisfy consumer demand for fur in a way that takes animal welfare into account:

- using the fur of invasive species that are non-native—and harmful—to a particular environment

- using the fur of roadkill
- selling vintage fur items, which allows someone to wear the fur of an animal that was killed decades ago rather than supporting companies that are killing more animals today

Whale Hunting

Commercial whalers have heavily hunted the great whales, such as blue, gray, right, and sperm whales, since the 1900s. Whale hunting has been widely condemned across the world, as it is in no way a sustainable practice. This hunting has had a huge impact on great whale populations, pushing many species to the edge of extinction. Recognizing the harmful impact of intensive commercial whaling, the International Whaling Commission (IWC) enacted an indefinite ban, known as a moratorium, on commercial whaling in 1985. This moratorium is supported by nearly all of the IWC's 87 member nations.

The countries of Norway and Iceland, however, have publicly objected to the moratorium and continue commercial whaling. They claim the hunt provides its citizens an opportunity to eat whale meat, a cultural tradition in those countries. Critics, however, claim the market for whale meat there has nearly disappeared and that practices cannot be allowed to continue simply because they are traditional.

Japan also hunts whales, claiming to do so for scientific research purposes, an activity legally allowed under the moratorium. According to Japan, their harvest of hundreds of whales each year provides data about whales, such as what they eat and how long they live. This information, they claim, will allow better management of whale and fishery resources. Critics say whales do not need to be killed to be studied. Additionally, because the whale meat is sold to restaurants and supermarkets, they say Japan's primary motive is clearly profit. However, Japan dismisses this accusation. Yuki Morita, a spokesman for the Whaling Division of the Ministry of Agriculture, Forestry and Fisheries in Tokyo, Japan, told international news website *DW* in 2017 "that all parts of the

An End to Foxhunting

Animal rights organizations claimed victory in 2004 when the British government banned the sport of foxhunting with dogs in England and Wales. For centuries, people have ridden horses behind packs of foxhounds as they followed the scent of a fox. A successful hunt ended as the hounds caught and killed their fox. According to animal rights activists who criticized the hunt, the fox's death was extremely inhumane as the pack of dogs ripped the living animal into pieces. Foxhunters disagreed. They claimed the fox would generally be killed by a single bite from one of the hounds.

As the new law took effect in early 2005, many members of foxhunting clubs condemned the action and staged vocal protests. Some even threatened to defy the ban. To them, hunting foxes with hounds is an age-old tradition that bonds members of the community. In addition, foxes are considered pest animals in rural Britain; hunts helped farmers rid their fields of the livestock predators.

Since being banned, traditional foxhunts have been replaced by "drag" hunts. In a drag hunt, a trail of fox scent is laid across the countryside. This compromise has caused discontent on both sides: Fox hunters tend to prefer the old style of hunting, while animal rights advocates still object to the fact that the foxes are killed. Several British prime ministers, including David Cameron and Theresa May, have stated that they would consider repealing the ban, but public support for this move has been too low for Parliament to bring the issue to a vote.

whale are used and the meat that is later sold on the market is to raise funds to cover the costs of the next year's research."[48]

In 2014, a ruling by the UN's International Court of Justice (ICJ) disputed that Japan's recent whaling expeditions had been done for scientific purposes and ordered them to halt their whaling operations. Japan initially complied but, as of 2018, has resumed whaling, although in significantly lower numbers than before, claiming that their whale hunting is done in a sustainable manner. They submitted their new plans to the ICJ but began operations without approval, as it is not required for both sides to approve the plan. Their new operations include the stipulation that they will not kill the whales unless sufficient scientific data cannot be obtained by nonlethal means. Despite this, Japanese whaling vessels killed more than 300 whales in 2017, leading to outrage among international activists.

AT GREATER RISK

"Three hundred thousand whales and dolphins drown in fishing nets each year and it is impossible to calculate how many more fall victim to pollution, ship strikes, the impacts of sonar or climate change ... How can pro-whaling nations justify hunting them as well?"

–Karen Sack, managing director of Ocean Unite, an ocean conservation organization

Quoted in "Threats to Whales and Dolphins Highlighted Around the World on Eve of Whaling Commission Meeting in Alaska," Greenpeace, accessed on May 14, 2018. www.greenpeace.org/usa/news/threats-to-whales-and-dolphins/

Animal rights activists object to commercial whale hunting for a variety of reasons. They, and many wildlife biologists, believe that populations of whales still recovering from the intensive hunting of earlier decades are not yet large enough to sustain hunting. In addition, other environmental factors such as pollution, ocean noise, fishing nets, collisions with ships, and global warming already place whale populations under enormous pressure. It has been extremely difficult and time consuming to bring back whale populations that have been driven to the edge of extinction, due to the fact that they have calves, or young whales, less frequently than other species and it takes a relatively long time for a calf to gestate, or develop in the womb. Hunting and killing whales only puts

While the International Whaling Commission has imposed a moratorium on commercial whaling, some countries have controversially continued their whaling operations.

the species under still more pressure. Finally, opponents of whaling also consider the practices that are often used to kill whales to be extremely inhumane. Whales shot by cannon-driven harpoons generally take many minutes to die. It is thought that whales experience a great deal of distress and suffering as they are pursued and killed.

Like many animal rights issues, whaling and the killing of other wildlife is a highly emotional issue that includes many different points of view. The variety of cultures, traditions, and values that impact these issues almost certainly guarantee that the debate will continue.

Controversy Over Animal Rights Activism Tactics

It is impossible to separate the facts of the treatment of animals by people from the emotions people have in response. Most people, quite understandably, react with shock and disgust to photos and descriptions of animals that suffer from mistreatment and abuse. Animal rights groups have tried to use the compassionate feelings most people have toward animals by specifically tailoring their messaging and media representation to pull at people's heartstrings. Many have become highly skilled at developing messages and creating sensational media events and slogans that use emotion to generate support for their point of view. These can range from playing an emotional song while showing images of neglected animals for a television commercial to depicting a fur coat stained with blood in a print advertisement.

Animal rights organizations are so skilled at delivering their messages that many of their ideas and practices have become widely accepted. This fact concerns those who believe that the general public fails to grasp the true motives of the animal rights movement. Writer and ethicist Wesley J. Smith explained,

> *We need to look past the public image of animal-rights/liberation groups, such as the People for the Ethical Treatment of Animals (PETA), as committed animal lovers who engage in wacky advocacy tactics such as posing nude to protest fur. For beneath this relatively benign façade lurks an ideologically absolutist movement that explicitly espouses equal moral worth between humans and animals. What's wrong with wanting to protect animals? Absolutely nothing. Indeed, advocating for animal welfare can be a noble cause. But this isn't the ultimate agenda of animal rights/liberation.*[49]

The Messaging of Animal Rights Groups

The ultimate agenda of animal rights groups is not always apparent to the casual supporter. Many people who seek to improve the welfare of animals and put an end to animal cruelty are unaware that many animal rights groups believe animals and people should be considered equals and that any use of animals by people for any reason is what they consider cruelty. Ingrid Newkirk, cofounder and president of PETA, illustrated this viewpoint when she famously stated, "There is no rational basis for saying that a human being has special rights. A rat is a pig is a dog is a boy."[50] Some animal rights groups also believe that every human use of animals should end, including the keeping of pets.

Of all the organizations advancing an extreme animal rights agenda, none has a higher profile than PETA. In 2017, the nonprofit organization received nearly $47 million in donations supporting its animal rights campaigns. PETA's website contains information on every aspect of the human use of animals and is viewed by more than 30 million people each year.

While PETA's campaigns are popular with some, their methods and those of other animal rights advocates, which attempt to force others to follow their beliefs, are often off-putting to others. In fact, many people connected to animal industries, as well as scientists, educators, and the general public, are concerned by the statements and tactics used by some of these groups to promote animal rights. One concern people have is that their positions are often seen as favoring animals over people. For example, Chris DeRose, founder of Last Chance for Animals, said, "If the death of one rat cured all diseases, it wouldn't make any difference to me."[51] Supporters do not see this as favoring animals over humans, but simply as treating animals and people in an equal fashion: If asked whether humans should be killed to find a cure for diseases, many people would say no. People are so accustomed to being able to use animals in whatever way they choose that true equality between species feels more favorable toward animals.

Additionally, animal rights campaigns use a variety of tactics to bring publicity to what they say are cases of animal abuse.

WHEN ACTIVISM MEETS VIOLENCE

"Animal rights activists engage in significant violence and lawlessness to coerce society into accepting their values."

–Wesley J. Smith, an attorney and author critical of animal rights extremists

Wesley J. Smith, "Four Legs Good, Two Legs Bad: The Anti-Human Values of 'Animal Rights,'" *Human Life Review*, Winter 2007, p. 7.

In his book, *Animal Rights: The Inhumane Crusade*, animal rights critic Daniel T. Oliver claimed that organizations may use unidentified or even fake photographs to portray cruelty to animals at the hands of trappers, farmers, or scientists. Oliver noted that another tactic is to portray isolated cases of animal mistreatment as typical throughout an industry. He added that an additional approach is to make unconfirmed or outright false claims of abuse to smear the reputations of people and businesses that conduct animal-related activities with which they disagree. Others have made the same accusations. According to the National Animal Interest Alliance (NAIA), an animal welfare organization, "we understand that animal cruelty exists, and we strongly condemn it. We also oppose the dishonest tactics used by some activists to paint some innocent people as abusers, and to change public policy by creating false perceptions."[52] The NAIA detailed several examples of videos created by animal rights groups that had been edited specifically to cause outrage. For instance, in 2010, the organization Mercy for Animals released a video showing terrible cruelty at an Ohio dairy farm. It was edited in such a way that the owner of the farm, Gary Conklin, appeared to be one of the abusers, but the truth was that he fired the abusive employee immediately upon learning about his actions. The NAIA said,

> *Despite an uproar in the media that included an open letter from [actress Jamie Lee Curtis], after seeing the entire, unedited video tape and hearing testimony from animal experts, a grand jury cleared Mr. Conklin of any charges of cruelty. The animal abuse*

> *captured on video was so obvious and egregious [terrible] that a mere 30 seconds of videotape would have been enough to get the violent worker fired and cited for cruelty, but disturbingly, Mercy for Animals allowed the torture to continue for weeks in its quest for more footage.*[53]

RATIONAL RIGHTS

"Rights are moral principles governing the interactions of rational, productive beings, who prosper not in a world of eat or be eaten, but a world of voluntary, mutually beneficial cooperation and trade."

–Alex Epstein, philosopher opposed to granting rights to animals

Alex Epstein, "The 'Animal Rights' Movement's Cruelty to Human Well Being," *New York Beacon*, August 25–31, 2005, p. 23.

Courting Outrage

PETA, in particular, is often accused of deliberately designing campaign messages with high shock value to win publicity, even if that publicity is negative. For two years, in 2003 and 2004, PETA toured college campuses and other venues with an exhibit promoting a vegetarian lifestyle. The campaign, called "Holocaust on Your Plate," argued that eating meat and wearing leather were morally the same as the murder of millions of Jews and other victims during the Holocaust. To make their point, PETA compared photos of chickens kept in factory farm cages to starving inmates of German concentration camps. Other images and exhibit text compared slaughtered animals to murdered Jews.

These comparisons caused outrage, especially among the Jewish community. "The effort by PETA to compare the deliberate, systematic murder of millions of Jews to the issue of animal rights is abhorrent,"[54] the Anti-Defamation League stated. Ethicist Wesley J. Smith agreed: "That PETA can't distinguish between the unspeakable evil of the Shoah [the Holocaust] and animal husbandry reveals a perverted sense of moral values that is almost beyond comprehension,"[55] he said.

PETA and other animal rights organizations often use emotionally charged images to get their point across.

Eventually PETA issued a half-hearted apology for the exhibit but went on to offend again the next year. This time, the exhibit, "Animal Liberation," compared the plight of animals to human slavery. Ads displayed images of the shackled foot of a black man next to that of a chained elephant. Another equated a seal being clubbed to a black civil rights protestor being beaten. One more compared a murdered black man with a cow in a slaughterhouse. The display toured 17 cities in 2005 before it was suspended due to public outcry.

"There is no comparison between criminal lynchings and the legal butchering of animals for food. There is no comparison between slaves and animals,"[56] said the National Association for the Advancement of Colored People (NAACP), condemning the exhibit. PETA spokesperson Dawn Carr defended their approach. "Every time you're challenging the status quo people will be upset … There is no question that the exhibits are difficult to look at … But it needs to be that way in order to break through the prejudice that exists," she said. "The purpose of this campaign is to point out that oppression and prejudice in any form is wrong."[57]

In 2017, PETA created a slightly less controversial campaign when they placed a billboard outside of Tulsa, Oklahoma, prior to the Christmas holiday. The ad featured a dog's head on a plate, taken from the dog meat trade in China, and questioned why people would eat a pig if they would not eat a dog.

According to PETA's website, the group uses these shock tactics deliberately. They operate on the belief that all press is good press, writing in their website FAQs:

> *PETA must rely largely on free "advertising" through media coverage. We will do extraordinary things to get the word out about animal cruelty because we have learned from experience that the media, sadly, do not consider the terrible facts about animal suffering alone interesting enough to cover. It is sometimes necessary to shake people up in order to initiate discussion, debate, questioning of the status quo, and, of course, action.*[58]

Escalating Tactics

Because some of the more extreme supporters of animal rights believe that the use of animals by people equates to slavery and murder, they justify the use of radical tactics to promote their views. They believe that, if people are to truly treat animals and human beings equally, transgressions against both must be punished equally. People would not stand for the systematic murder and enslavement of other human beings, so animal activists ask, why would they allow it among animals? In some cases, these tactics are not just controversial, they are illegal. Increasingly, animal research facilities, animal researchers, and animal agriculture facilities are becoming the targets of vandalism, harassment, and even threats of violence and death. Many of these activities are carried out by people working in a loose network of underground activists, often under the banner of the Animal Liberation Front (ALF).

The ALF began in the United Kingdom in the 1970s and started operations in the United States in the 1980s. It now has operatives working in many other countries. According to the ALF website, its movement "carries out direct action against animal abuse in the form of rescuing animals and causing financial loss to animal exploiters, usually through the damage and destruction of property ... It is a nonviolent campaign, activists taking all precautions not to harm

A Dangerous Suggestion

Although many of PETA's suggestion are extreme, most are not actively harmful. For instance, the idea that people should stop eating meat is unpopular, but a carefully managed vegetarian or vegan diet will not cause health problems for people. However, PETA also advocates a vegetarian or vegan diet for pet cats and dogs. The organization has several claims to support this view:

- A diet high in meat is unhealthy for animals the same way it is unhealthy for humans.
- Most pet food is made with meat such as chicken or beef, which supports the cruelty of the meat industry.
- Allowing cats and dogs to hunt animals such as mice or birds for themselves, as they would in the wild, is unfair to the prey because being kept as a pet gives the predator an unnatural advantage.

Veterinarians agree that the first statement is false; in fact, the opposite is true. Dogs and cats need meat in their diets to keep them healthy. According to veterinarian Dr. Karen Becker, "Dogs are scavenging carnivores. In general terms this means they are primarily meat-eaters, but can survive on plant material alone if necessary. The key word here is 'survive' ... To thrive is to grow vigorously ... To survive means simply to stay alive."[1] In other words, while a dog may not die if it is fed only vegan food, it will likely not be very healthy. Cats need nutrients that are difficult to get in sufficient amounts from foods other than meat, even when supplements are added to the diet. Veterinary nutritionist Cailin Heinze said, "For cats, [a vegetarian or vegan diet is] really inappropriate. It goes against their physiology and isn't something I would recommend at all."[2] People who want a pet but do not want to support the meat industry by buying meat-based pet food can get naturally vegan pets such as fish or rabbits.

1. Karen Becker, "The Alarming New Vegan Pet Food Branded by Celebrity Ellen DeGeneres," Healthy Pets, January 19, 2012. healthypets.mercola.com/sites/healthypets/archive/2012/01/19/vegetarianism-for-pets.aspx
2. Quoted in Elizabeth Kulze, "PETA's Most Outrageously Dishonest Ad Campaigns," Vocativ, June 2, 2014. www.vocativ.com/culture/science/petas-outrageously-dishonest-ad-campaigns/.

any animal (human or otherwise)."[59] ALF's actions are undertaken by individuals working alone or in small, loosely organized groups targeting anyone they feel abuses or exploits animals. Actions have included the release of animals, theft, arson, and vandalism. Targets have included animal research facilities, research animal breeding farms, and farms raising animals for the fur industry. In one incident, an ALF member called a hotel and threatened to burn it down if the restaurant did not stop serving rabbit and other specific food items.

A report compiled by the Foundation for Biomedical Research in Washington, D.C., found that worldwide, there were 88 ALF incidents in the 1980s, 132 in the 1990s, and 363 incidents from 2000 to 2005. They reached their height in the early 2000s, but more effective, efficient policing and a better understanding of how to track and monitor internet activity has led to a decrease in the last 10 years. In 2004, the Federal Bureau of Investigation (FBI) testified before the Senate Judiciary Committee that since 1976, the ALF had caused about $110 million in damage. The FBI has classified it as a domestic terrorist organization.

The Animal Liberation Front is an extreme animal rights organization that targets businesses and individuals its members feel harm animals. The group's goal is to shut them down by any means necessary.

Not all ALF members follow the group's stated nonviolent ideology. In one case, a bomb aimed at a researcher studying primate behavior was left at the wrong house. Although it failed to explode, it was powerful enough to have destroyed the home, occupied by a 70-year-old woman. In another case, University of California, Los Angeles (UCLA) neurobiology professor Dario Ringach announced his decision to halt his primate research after years of threats to his family. Ringach sent an email to the ALF reading, "You win. Effective immediately, I am no longer doing animal research."[60]

"WHATEVER MEANS NECESSARY"

"I think people who torture innocent beings should be stopped. If they won't stop when you ask them nicely, they don't stop when you demonstrate to them what they're doing is wrong, then they should be stopped using whatever means necessary."

–Dr. Jerry Vlasak, Animal Liberation Front spokesperson

Quoted in Steve Hymon, "Animal Rights Leader Justifies Violence," *Los Angeles Times*, November 13, 2005. articles.latimes.com/2005/nov/13/local/me-vlasak13.

A Fundamental Difference in Beliefs

Unfortunately, it is very difficult to see any kind of common ground on the subject of animal rights. As animal rights activists become more adamant that animals are as deserving of rights as people, traditionalists will continue to dig in their heels, insisting that human beings, as the only species able to think and reason, are superior over all other species. As it stands right now, this is not a bridgeable gap. This is a fundamental difference in beliefs. Animal rights advocate Michael Tobias acknowledged the range of opinions that exist on the subject. "It is fair, and necessary, to acknowledge myriad grays in between the worlds of meat eating and vegetarianism, between those who would demand no human being ever exploit any animal … and those who find such points-of-view to be extreme or, at the very least, impractical,"[61] he wrote.

Deborah Rudacille, a former researcher at the Johns Hopkins Center for Alternatives to Animal Testing, believes that despite their conflicting viewpoints concerning the treatment of animals, people on both sides of the

ONE BAD APPLE SPOILS THE BUNCH

"Just as the pro-life movement is haunted by the murderers of abortion doctors, the environmental and animal-rights movements are cursed by their own packs of fierce radicals."

–John J. Miller, political reporter for the *National Review*

John J. Miller, "In the Name of Animals," *National Review*, July 3, 2006, p. 38.

issue must ultimately respect each individual's opinion on the matter:

> *The very fact that we are able to entertain these questions at all points to a key difference between human beings and other animals. Whether that difference is profound enough to enable us to continue to use animals as food, as experimental subjects, as the means to our ends, is something that each of us must contemplate and decide in the private space of individual conscience—recognizing that our answer to that question may well conflict with those of other people of good will and conscience. This ambiguous [unclear] and unsettling outcome may be the best that we can hope for until our unquenchable human ingenuity finds a path beyond the conflict and a solution to which all can, in good conscience, agree.*[62]

NOTES

Introduction: Understanding the Controversy

1. Quoted in David Favre, "Overview of Historical Animal Law Materials," Michigan State University College of Law, Animal Legal and Historical Center, 2002. www.animallaw.info/historical/articles/ovushistory.htm#The%20British%20Set%20the%20Stage.

Chapter 1: Animal Rights

2. Immanuel Kant, *Kant: The Metaphysics of Morals (Cambridge Texts in the History of Philosophy)*. Cambridge, UK: Cambridge University Press, 1996.
3. *The Law Quarterly Review*, vol. XVIII, ed. Sir Frederick Pollock. London, UK: Stevens and Sons, Limited, 1902, p. 34.
4. Gary L. Francione, *Introduction to Animal Rights: Your Child or the Dog?* Philadelphia, PA: Temple University Press, 2000, p. xxv.
5. Francione, *Introduction to Animal Rights*, p. xxix.
6. Francione, *Introduction to Animal Rights*, p. xxxiv.
7. Quoted in Matthew Scully, *Dominion*. New York, NY: St. Martin's, 2002, p. 6.
8. Marc Bekoff, *The Emotional Lives of Animals*. Novato, CA: New World Library, 2007, p. 134.
9. Francione, *Introduction to Animal Rights*, p. 141.
10. Jane Goodall, foreword to *The Emotional Lives of Animals*, p. xiii.
11. Leland Shapiro, *Applied Animal Ethics*. New York, NY: Delmar Thomson Learning, 2000, p. 153.

12. Shapiro, *Applied Animal Ethics*, p. 154.

13. Richard A. Epstein, "The Next Rights Revolution?," *National Review*, November 8, 1999. findarticles.com/p/articles/mi_m1282/is_ 21_51/ai_56899764.

14. Tia Ghose, "Animals Are Moral Creatures, Scientist Argues," LiveScience, November 15, 2012. www.livescience.com/24802-animals-have-morals-book.html.

15. Quoted in Daniel T. Oliver, *Animal Rights: The Inhumane Crusade*. Bellevue, WA: Capital Research Center, 1999, p. xiv.

16. Quoted in Richard Ryder, "Discrimination on the Basis of Species is Unjust," *The Rights of Animals*. San Diego, CA: Greenhaven, 1999, p. 26.

Chapter 2: Farm Animals

17. Richard W. Bulliet, *Hunters, Herders, and Hamburgers*. New York, NY: Columbia University Press, 2005, p. 3.

18. Yuzhi Li and Lee Johnston, "Research Reaffirms the Necessity of Tail Docking for Pigs," *National Hog Farmer*, December 30, 2016. www.nationalhogfarmer.com/animal-welfare/research-reaffirms-necessity-tail-docking-pigs.

19. Gaverick Matheny and Kai M. A. Chan, "Human Diets and Animal Welfare: The Illogic of the Larder," *Journal of Agricultural and Environmental Ethics*, 2005, vol. 18, pp. 581–582.

20. Shapiro, *Applied Animal Ethics*, p. 172.

21. Quoted in Joby Warrick, "They Die Piece by Piece," *Washington Post*, April 10, 2001. www.washingtonpost.com/archive/politics/2001/04/10/they-die-piece-by-piece/f172dd3c-0383-49f8-b6d8-347e04b68da1/?utm_term=.b20a5a2b39f3.

22. Quoted in Warrick, "They Die Piece by Piece."

23. Temple Grandin, "Progress and Challenges in Animal

Handling and Slaughter in the U.S.," *Applied Animal Behavior Science*, 2006, pp. 129–139. www.grandin.com/references/progress.challenges.us.animal.handling.html.

24. Francione, *Introduction to Animal Rights*, p. 188.

Chapter 3: Animals as Test Subjects

25. C. Ray Greek and Jean Swingle Greek, *Sacred Cows and Golden Geese*. New York, NY: Continuum, 2000, pp. 17–18.

26. Miriam Wells, "Inside the Monkey Lab: The Ethics of Testing on Animals," *Vice News*, July 7, 2015. news.vice.com/article/inside-the-monkey-lab-the-ethics-of-testing-on-animals.

27. "Alternatives to Animal Testing," PETA, accessed on May 2, 2018. www.peta.org/issues/animals-used-for-experimentation/alternatives-animal-testing/.

28. Teal Burrell, "Can We Eliminate Animals from Medical Research?," *NOVA Next*, August 7, 2013. www.pbs.org/wgbh/nova/next/body/eliminating-animal-models/.

29. "Alternatives to Animal Testing," PETA.

Chapter 4: Animals as Entertainment

30. Quoted in Tracy Wilkinson, "Rebirth in the Arena," *Los Angeles Times*, October 16, 2007, p. A1.

31. Quoted in Wilkinson, "Rebirth in the Arena," p. A1.

32. Quoted in Dan Bilefsky, "Matador Wins. Bull Dies. The End? Not in Portugal," *New York Times*, August 12, 2007, p. A10.

33. Quoted in "Spain Bullfighting: Thousands Rally in Madrid to Demand Bullfighting Ban," BBC, September 10, 2016. www.bbc.com/news/world-europe-37329315.

34. "A Closer Look at Dogfighting," ASPCA, accessed on May 2, 2018. www.aspca.org/animal-cruelty/dog-fighting/closer-look-dogfighting.

35. Quoted in Christina M. Russo, "Michael Vick May Have Actually Made Dogfighting More Popular," *The Dodo*, January 21, 2016. www.thedodo.com/michael-vick-dogfighting-more-popular-1565236921.html.

36. Quoted in Paul Duggan, "A Blood Sport Exposed," *Washington Post*, August 22, 2007, p. A1.

37. Quoted in Larry Silver, "Activists Protest Animal Treatment; Rodeo Defends Actions," *Arizona Daily Star*, February 28, 2004. www.fox11az.com/news/local/stories/022804ccktFOX11Rodeo.3a729a44.html#.

38. Quoted in George Vecsey, "Sports of the Times; Racing Can't Afford More Tragedies," *New York Times*, June 6, 1993. query.nytimes.com/gst/fullpage.html?res=9F0CE7D81E3DF935A35755C0A965958260.

39. Quoted in George Vecsey, "Psychic Pull of an Injured Racehorse," *New York Times*, May 24, 2006. www.nytimes.com/2006/05/24/sports/othersports/24vecsey.html?mtrref=www.google.com&gwh=3ECE927D9669F28DE3D7A8FCB2845605&gwt=pay.

Chapter 5: Animal Rights in the Wild

40. "Why Sport Hunting Is Cruel and Unnecessary," PETA, accessed on May 3, 2018. www.peta.org/issues/wildlife/wildlife-factsheets/sport-hunting-cruel-unnecessary/.

41. "Where Does the Money for Conservation Come From?," Montana Hunter's Ed Course, accessed on May 3, 2018. www.hunter-ed.com/montana/studyGuide/Where-Does-the-Money-for-Conservation-Come-From/201027_700048372/.

42. Thomas P. Rooney, "What Do We Do with Too Many White-Tailed Deer?," Action Bioscience, May 2010. www.actionbioscience.org/biodiversity/rooney.html.

43. Quoted in Michael Satchell, "A View to a Kill: How Safari Club Int'l Works to Weaken ESA Protections,"

Humane Society of the United States, November 25, 2003. www.hsus.org/archive/about_us/about_hsus_programs_and_services/eye_on_the_opposition/a_view_to_a_kill_how_safari_club_intl_works_to_weaken_esa_protections.html.

44. Quoted in Satchell, "A View to a Kill."

45. "Safari Club International: Frequently Asked Questions," Humane Society of the United States, last updated June 10, 2011. www.humanesociety.org/issues/opposition/facts/safari_club_faq.html.

46. Norimitsu Onishi, "Outcry for Cecil the Lion Could Undercut Conservation Efforts," *New York Times*, August 10, 2015. www.nytimes.com/2015/08/11/world/africa/outcry-for-cecil-the-lion-could-undercut-conservation-efforts.html.

47. Jenni Avins, "There's Actually a Way to Feel Good About Wearing Fur," Quartz, March 6, 2015. qz.com/356854/theres-actually-a-way-to-feel-good-about-fur/.

48. Quoted in Julian Ryall, "How Does Japan Get Away with 'Horrific' Whale Hunting?," *DW*, November 30, 2017. www.dw.com/en/how-does-japan-get-away-with-horrific-whale-hunting/a-41596992.

Chapter 6: Controversy Over Animal Rights Activism Tactics

49. Wesley J. Smith, "Four Legs Good, Two Legs Bad: The Anti-Human Values of 'Animal Rights,'" *Human Life Review*, Winter 2007, p. 8.

50. Quoted in Smith, "Four Legs Good, Two Legs Bad," p. 9.

51. Quoted in Alex Epstein, "The 'Animal Rights' Movement's Cruelty to Human Well-Being," *New York Beacon*, August 25–31, 2005, p. 23.

52. Staff, "Deception in the Name of Animal Rights," National Animal Interest Alliance, last updated 2017.

www.naiaonline.org/articles/article/deception-in-the-name-of-animal-rights#sthash.opF6Zls7.dpbs.

53. Staff, "Deception in the Name of Animal Rights."

54. Quoted in Zenitha Prince, "PETA Generates Outrage; Equating Blacks with Mistreated Animals," *Afro-American*, August 27–September 2, 2005, p. A1.

55. Quoted in Prince, "PETA Generates Outrage," p. A1.

56. Quoted in Prince, "PETA Generates Outrage," p. A1.

57. Quoted in Prince, "PETA Generates Outrage," p. A1.

58. "Why Does PETA Use Controversial Tactics?," PETA, accessed on May 4, 2018. www.peta.org/about-peta/faq/why-does-peta-use-controversial-tactics/.

59. "The ALF Credo and Guidelines," Animal Liberation Front, accessed on May 4, 2018. animalliberationfront.com/ALFront/alf_credo.htm.

60. Quoted in Rebecca Trounson and Joe Mozingo, "UCLA to Protect Animal Research," *Los Angeles Times*, August 26, 2006. articles.latimes.com/2006/aug/26/local/me-ucla26.

61. Michael Tobias, *Voices from the Underground*. Pasadena, CA: New Paradigm, 1999, p. 27.

62. Deborah Rudacille, *The Scalpel and the Butterfly: The War Between Animal Research and Animal Protection*. New York, NY: Farrar, Straus and Giroux, 2000, pp. 312–313.

DISCUSSION QUESTIONS

Chapter 1: Animal Rights

1. Explain the difference between animal welfare and animal rights. Which do you support?
2. How does Marc Bekoff's statement that well-being does not center on what animals know, but rather what they feel, relate to the suffering of animals?
3. Why do you think people are more willing to extend basic rights to household pets, such as cats and dogs, than they are to other animals, such as chickens or rats?

Chapter 2: Farm Animals

1. In your opinion, does the need to produce inexpensive and abundant food justify the conditions of animals raised on factory farms?
2. Would you choose or have you chosen to become vegetarian or vegan? Why or why not?
3. What are some ways you can keep animal welfare or animal rights in mind when choosing your food?

Chapter 3: Animals as Test Subjects

1. Do you think it is necessary for researchers to do experiments on animals? Why or why not?
2. Should students be required to dissect animals in the classroom? Why or why not?
3. How does the set of guiding principles known as the Three Rs govern the treatment of laboratory animals? Do you think these guidelines are adequate?

Chapter 4: Animals as Entertainment

1. Do you believe bullfighting is cruel? Why or why not?
2. Why does dogfighting continue to be practiced in the United States?
3. Do you believe it is wrong to use animals in non-blood sports, such as racing and rodeo events? Why or why not?

Chapter 5: Animal Rights in the Wild

1. Do you agree with hunting for recreation, for trophies, or for fur? Explain your answer.
2. Why do you think the number of hunters has decreased in recent years?
3. Is it okay to hunt some wild animals but not others? Explain your answer.

Chapter 6: Controversy Over Animal Rights Activism Tactics

1. Do you think animal rights organizations are honest about their motives? If so, why? If not, why not?
2. Do you agree with the tactics groups such as PETA and the ALF use? Why or why not?
3. Should extreme animal rights activists who engage in illegal activities be considered terrorists? Why or why not?

ORGANIZATIONS TO CONTACT

American Anti-Vivisection Society (AAVS)
801 Old York Rd., Suite 204
Jenkintown, PA 19046
(800) 729-2287
aavs@aavs.org
www.aavs.org

The AAVS opposes experiments on living animals and promotes alternative research methods. The organization produces videos, magazines, and brochures.

American Association for Laboratory Animal Science (AALAS)
9190 Crestwyn Hills Dr
Memphis, TN 38125
(901) 754-8620
www.aalas.org

The AALAS is a professional organization devoted to the care and study of animals used in medical research. It provides seminars and publications for lab animal technicians as well as a technician-certification program.

Animal Welfare Institute (AWI)
900 Pennsylvania Avenue SE
Washington, DC 20003
(202) 337-2332
awionline.org

AWI works to reduce the suffering of animals used in agriculture and research—for instance, by replacing factory farms with humane, family-run farms. It also campaigns against brutal methods of fur trapping and for protection of wildlife.

Humane Society of the United States (HSUS)
1255 23rd Street NW, Suite 450
Washington, DC 20037
(202) 452-1100
www.hsus.org

Established in 1954, the HSUS is the country's largest animal protection organization. Its programs cover a wide variety of animal issues, including promoting the humane treatment of animals in agriculture and research.

People for the Ethical Treatment of Animals (PETA)
501 Front Street
Norfolk, VA 23510
(757) 622-7382
www.peta.org

PETA claims to be the world's largest animal rights organization. It uses public education, cruelty investigations, legislation, celebrity involvement, and protest campaigns to bring attention to the uses of animals on factory farms, in laboratories, in the clothing trade, and in the entertainment industry.

FOR MORE INFORMATION

Books

Abramovitz, Melissa. *Thinking Critically: Animal Rights*. San Diego, CA: ReferencePoint Press, Inc, 2018.

This book examines debates about animal rights that affect industries as diverse as entertainment, biomedical research, and food service.

Grandin, Temple, and Catherine Johnson. *Animals in Translation: Using the Mysteries of Autism to Decode Animal Behavior*. San Diego, CA: Harcourt, 2006.

Respected animal scientist Temple Grandin has said that her autism makes her better able to understand the way animals think. In this book, she describes what animal consciousness is like and states that they are just as intelligent as humans, but with different skills.

Perdew, Laura. *Animal Rights Movement*. North Mankato, MN: ABDO Publishing Company, 2014.

The author examines various aspects of the animal rights movement.

Woods, Bob. *Animal Testing: Attacking a Controversial Problem*. Broomall, PA: Mason Crest, 2018.

Some people believe animal testing is necessary, while others think it should be banned. This book examines both sides of the issue.

Websites

Americans for Medical Progress (AMP)
www.amprogress.org

This organization provides information on the use of animals in medical research. The website also provides counterpoints to claims made by animal rights organizations against animal research.

Animal Legal and Historical Center, Michigan State University College of Law
www.animallaw.info

This comprehensive website contains a catalog of laws and legal cases relating to animals in the United States and around the world. Visitors can search for laws by topic, animal species, state, or country.

Humane Farming Association (HFA)
www.hfa.org

This organization is dedicated to reducing cruelty to farm animals and ending the practice of factory farming.

In Defense of Animals (IDA)
www.idausa.org

In Defense of Animals campaigns against animal abuse and cruelty and advocates for ending the property status of animals.

National Animal Interest Alliance (NAIA)
www.naiaonline.org

NAIA is dedicated to promoting animal welfare through programs that find loving homes for animals, as well as protecting the rights of pet owners. It also aims to educate the public about the difference between animal rights and animal welfare.

INDEX

PICTURE CREDITS

Cover Himanshuroy Fulwala/EyeEm/Getty Images; p. 7 Miriam Doerr Martin Frommherz/Shutterstock.com; p. 10 Corbis/Corbis via Getty Images; p. 13 bernatets photo/Shutterstock.com; p. 16 ZSSD/Minden Pictures/Minden Pictures/Getty Images; p. 20 John Zich/The LIFE Images Collection/Getty Images; p. 22 Chelsea Lauren/FilmMagic/Getty Images; p. 25 Courtesy of Statista.com; p. 28 Edwin Remsburg/VW Pics via Getty Images; p. 31 Judd Christie Photography/Moment/Getty Images; p. 35 Roma Black/Shutterstock.com; p. 38 Igor Smirnoff/Shutterstock.com; p. 41 Aaron Haupt/Science Source/Getty Images; p. 44 PATRICK HERTZOG/AFP/Getty Images; p. 48 David Tadevosian/Shutterstock.com; p. 51 Hulton Archive/Getty Images; p. 55 Yann Guichaoua-Photos/Moment Unreleased/Getty Images; p. 59 photo-denver/Shutterstock.com; p. 64 Mitch Kezar/Design Pics/Getty Images; p. 66 FotoRequest/Shutterstock.com; p. 68 S.J. Krasemann/Photodisc/Getty Images; p. 71 Barcroft Media/Barcroft Media via Getty Images; p. 72 Dmitry Abaza/Shutterstock.com; p. 76 Yann hubert/Shutterstock.com; p. 81 MANJUNATH KIRAN/AFP/Getty Images; p. 84 PA Images via Getty Images.

ABOUT THE AUTHOR

Tyler Stevenson is a professional in the health insurance industry. He graduated from the University at Buffalo with a degree in sociology and originally went into banking before making the switch to health insurance. He works in Buffalo, New York, and lives in the City of Tonawanda with his wife; his two young daughters, Autumn and Summer; his dog; his two cats; and the family guinea pig, Pig-Pig.